the
sock report
FOR THE LOVE OF SOCK YARN

edited by Janel Laidman

Photographs ©2012, Benjamin Wheeler and Rustling Leaf Press

ISBN-13: 978-0-9814972-5-9

a midsummer's dream

marigold

Susanna IC

suki

Miriam **Pike**

blomster

AnneLena **Mattison**

clio

Snowden **Becker**

tulip dreams

AnneLena **Mattison**

pocket pals

Chris deLongpré

Curiouser & Curiouser

" and how funny it'll seem, sending presents to one's own feet! And how odd the directions will look!

Alice's Right Foot, Esq.,
Hearthrug,
Near the Fender.
(with Alice's Love)

"

- Lewis Carroll

devonian

Laura Kanemori

semadar

Heatherly **Walker**

cambium

Kristi **Geraci**

wanderlust

Friederike **Erbslein**

phaedaria

Hunter **Hammersen**

the cure for anything

> "the cure for anything is salt water;
> sweat, tears or the sea"
>
> -Isak Dineson

Arcadia

Janel Laidman

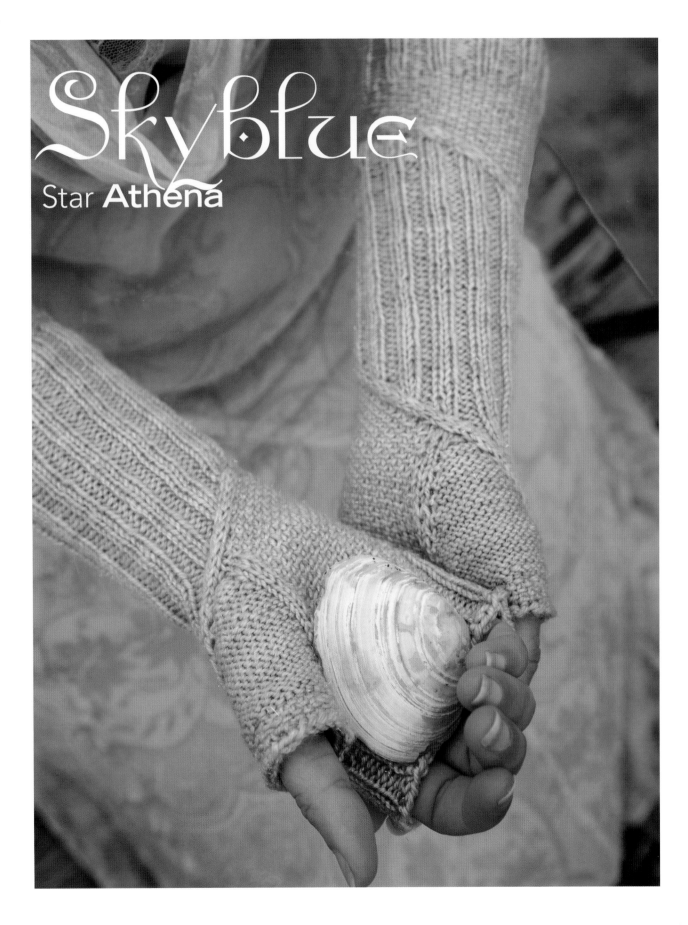

Zigzag Wanderer

Kimley Maretzo

Bivalve

Kirsten Kapur

Cassian

Corrina **Ferguson**

Patterns

1. MARIGOLD

sizes One size; gauge and blocking will affect size.

yarn Fingering weight sock yarn, approximately 866 yds (792 m).

Sample shown in Socktopus Sokkusu (100% superwash merino wool), 433 yds (396 m) per 120 g in color "Slice of Orange," 2 skeins.

needles Recommended: US 6 (4 mm) circular or straight needle, or size needed to obtain gauge.

Circular or straight needle for bind-off in two sizes larger than main needle.

gauge 4.5 stitches / 6 rows per inch (2.5 cm) in stockinette worked flat. Correct gauge is not critical for this project, but your final measurements and yardage requirements may vary if your gauge is different.

notions Approximately 250 size 5/0 (4.5mm) beads (optional). Size 14 (0.75 mm) crochet hook or size small enough to fit through hole of beads (optional). Scrap yarn for provisional cast-on, tapestry needle.

pattern notes The wrap is worked seamlessly from a center temporary cast-on down to both ends. The main body is a simple and quick-to-knit leaf lace, which contrasts nicely with the more elaborate border stitches. Optional beading along the edges makes a pretty addition to the knit and adds extra weight and interest to the finished shawl.

Bead Placement The beads are placed using a slender steel crochet hook. To place a bead on a stitch, insert the hook through the hole in the bead and slide the bead up onto the hook. Pick the stitch off the needle with the hook and slide the bead down onto the stitch. Slip the stitch back to left needle and knit it.

cast-on With scrap yarn and smaller needle, cast on 77 stitches using a provisional cast-on. Attach project yarn, knit one row, then purl one row.

Chart 1

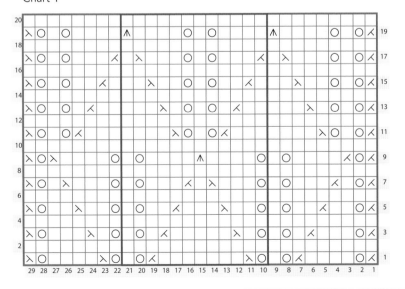

	k on RS, p on WS
⟍	k2tog
⟋	ssk
⋀	cdd
O	yo
•	optional bead placement
⟍	k3tog
⟋	sssk

Chart 2 (first half)

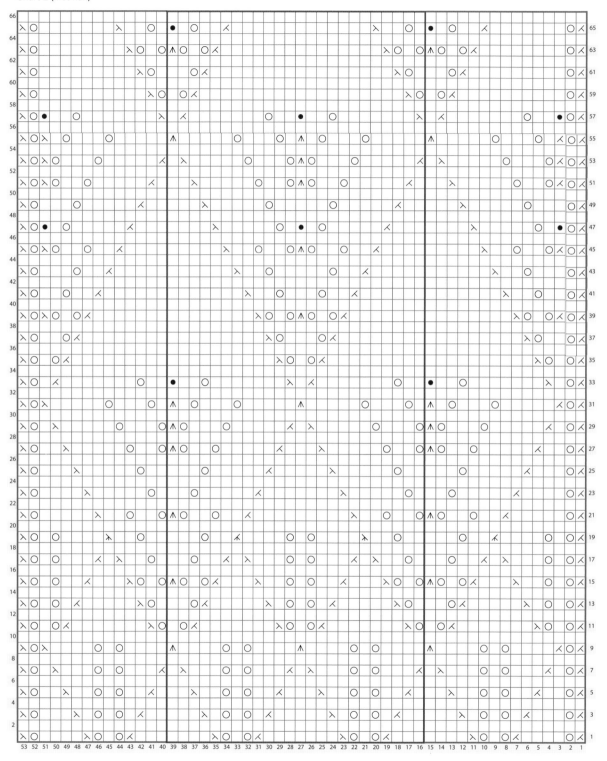

Chart 2 (second half)

first half of body Work first half of shawl as follows (purl all WS rows): Work chart 1 (rows 1 – 20) seven times.

Work chart 2 (rows 1 – 127) one time.

bind off first half Switch to larger needle to bind off next WS row.

Bind-off row (WS): P2, [return both stitches to left needle, p2tog, p1], repeat to end.

second half of body Carefully remove the provisional cast-on placing live stitches, with wrong side facing, on smaller needle. Attach project yarn; purl 1 row.

Work second half of shawl same as first.

bind off second half Switch to larger needle to bind off next WS row.

Bind off in the same manner as the first half.

finishing Weave in ends, block on mat.

2. SUKI

sizes Small (large). Gauge and blocking will affect final size. Sample shown in size large.

yarn Fingering weight sock yarn, approximately 300 (400) yds (274 (366) m) of color A (main color) and 200 (250) yds (183 (229) m) of color B (contrast color).

Sample shown in Textiles a Mano Caricia (80% superwash merino wool, 10% cashmere, 10% nylon), 458 yds (418 m) per 113 g in colors "Sage Leaf"(color A) and "Mostly Moss" (color B), 1 skein of each.

needles Recommended: US 5 (3.75 mm) circular needle, 32", or size needed to obtain gauge.

gauge 5 stitches / 9 rows per inch (2.5 cm) in stockinette worked flat, after blocking. Correct gauge is not critical for this project but your final measurements and yardage requirements may vary if your gauge is different.

notions Stitch markers, tapestry needle.

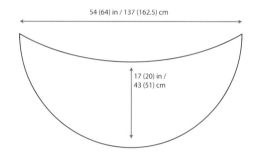

54 (64) in / 137 (162.5) cm

17 (20) in / 43 (51) cm

garter tab cast-on With color A, cast on three stitches. Knit 7 rows, slipping the first stitch of every row as if to purl with yarn in front. Turn 90 degrees and pick up three stitches in to the side of your work and then three stitches into your cast on stitches [9 stitches total]. Turn, ready to begin set up rows:

setup NOTE: *The first stitch is always slipped purlwise, with yarn in front.*

Row 1 (WS): Slip 1, k2, yo, p2, place marker, p1, yo, k3 [11 stitches].

body section
Row 1 (RS): Slip 1, k2, yo, knit until marker, m1R, slip marker, k1, m1L, knit to last three stitches, yo, k3.
Row 2: Slip 1, k2, yo, purl to last three stitches, yo, k3.
Row 3: Slip 1, k2, yo, knit to last three stitches, yo, k3.
Row 4: Slip 1, k2, yo, purl to last three stitches, yo, k3.

Repeat these 4 rows until you have 111 (171) stitches on the needle, having just finished row 4.

stripe section

Row 1 (color A): Slip 1, k2, yo, knit until marker, m1R, slip marker, k1, m1L, knit to last three stitches, yo, k3.

Row 2 (color B): Slip 1, k2, yo, purl to last three stitches, yo, k3.

Row 3 (color B): Slip 1, k2, yo, purl to last three stitches, yo, k3.

Row 4 (color B): Slip 1, k2, yo, purl to last three stitches, yo, k3.

Row 5 (color B): Slip 1, k2, yo, k1, [yo, k2tog] repeat between [] to marker, yo, slip marker, k1, yo, [k2tog, yo] repeat between [] to last 4 stitches, k1, yo, k3.

Row 6 (color B): Slip 1, k2, yo, purl to last three stitches, yo, k3.

Row 7 (color B): Slip 1, k2, yo, purl to last three stitches, yo, k3.

Row 8 (color A): Slip 1, k2, yo, purl to last three stitches, yo, k3.

[20 stitches increased each time rows 1-8 are repeated.]

Repeat these 8 rows (carrying your unused color up the side of your work) until you have 235 (295) stitches, having just finished row 1 [6 contrast color stripes for both sizes].

For small only:

Using color B, work 4 purl rows in the following manner:

Row 1 (WS): Slip 1, k2 yo, purl to last 3, yo k3.
Row 2: Slip 1, k2, yo, purl to last 3, yo, k3.
Row 3: Slip 1, k2, yo, purl to last 3, yo, k3.
Row 4: Slip 1 k2, yo, purl to marker, m1Rp, slip marker, p1, m1Lp, purl to last 3, yo, k3.

Change color back to A and work row 5 in this manner:

Row 5: Slip 1, k2, yo, purl to last 3, yo, k3.

For large only:

Next Row: Using color A, slip 1, k2, purl to last 3, k3.

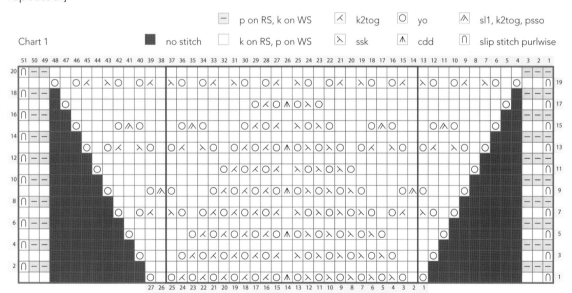

Chart 1

Chart 2

Note:
The stitches within the red boxes are the chart repeat. On Chart 2, work repeat to last 34 stitches. End working stitches 4-34, then k3.

For both sizes: Cut color B, leaving a tail to weave in then continue to lace pattern. [247 (295) stitches].

lace section

Chart 1

Work chart 1, repeating the stitches in the red box 10 (12) times until chart is complete.

Chart 2

Work chart 2, repeating the stitches in the red box to last 34 stitches. End working stitches 4-34 (one repeat less the final cdd), then k3.

Next Row (WS): Slip 1, k2, yo, purl to last 3, yo, k3.

bind-off Change to color B. Knit 2 rows then work the picot bind-off as follows: Using the knitted cast-on, [cast on 2, bind off 5 place last stitch back on left needle] repeat to end.

finishing Weave in ends, pinning out picots, block on mat.

3. BLOMSTER

sizes Small (medium, large).

yarn Fingering weight sock yarn, approximately 436 yds (399 m).

Sample shown in Lorna's Laces Shepherd Sock (80% superwash merino wool, 20% nylon), 436 yds (399 m) per 100 g in color "Valentine."

needles US 1.5 (2.5 mm) dpns or circular needle, or size needed to obtain gauge.

gauge 8 stitches / 12 rows per inch (2.5 cm) in stockinette worked in the round.

notions Stitch markers, tapestry needle.

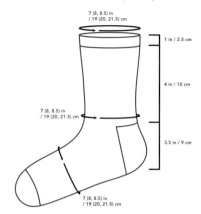

cast-on Cast on 28 stitches using Judy's Magic Cast-On (14 sole stitches, 14 instep stitches).

toe

Round 1:
Sole: K1, kfb, knit to last 2 stitches, kfb, k1.
Instep: Repeat sole stitches.

Round 2: Knit.

Repeat rounds 1 and 2 until there are 60 (64, 68) total stitches: 30 (32, 34) instep stitches, 30 (32, 34) sole stitches.

foot

Round 1:
Sole: Knit.
Instep: [Yo, k2tog] repeat to end.

Rounds 2-3: Knit.

Round 4:
Sole: Knit.
Instep: K4 (5, 6), work chart 1, k4, work chart 1, k4 (5,6).

Repeat round 4 until sock measures 3.5 inches (9 cm) less than total foot measurement.

gusset
Round 1 (increase round):
Sole: K1, kfb, knit to last 2 stitches, kfb, k1.
Instep: K4 (5, 6), work chart, k4, work chart, k4 (5,6).

Round 2: Work even in pattern.

Repeat these two rounds 16 times total [92 (96, 100) stitches: 62 (64, 66) sole/heel stitches, 30 (32, 34) instep stitches].

heel turn
Set instep stitches aside; only sole/heel stitches will be worked back and forth. Place markers on sole after stitches 17 and 45 (47, 49).

Row 1 (RS): K44 (46, 48), wrap and turn.
Row 2 (WS): P26 (28, 30), wrap and turn.
Row 3: K24 (26, 28), wrap and turn.
Row 4: P22 (24, 26), wrap and turn.
Row 5: K20 (22, 24), wrap and turn.
Row 6: P18 (20, 22), wrap and turn.
Row 7: K16 (18, 20), wrap and turn.
Row 8: P14 (16, 18), wrap and turn.
Row 9: K12 (14, 16), wrap and turn.
Row 10: P10 (12, 14), wrap and turn.
Row 11: K8 (10, 12), wrap and turn.
Row 12: Purl across to marker, purling wraps together with their wrapped stitches; remove marker, p2tog. Turn; this leaves a gap.
Row 13: Slip 1 purlwise, knit across to marker, knitting wraps together with their wrapped stitches; remove marker, ssk. Turn; this leaves a gap.

heel flap
You will now work back and forth on the middle 30 (32, 34) heel stitches, while slowly decreasing the gusset stitches.

Row 1 (WS): Slip 1 purlwise, purl to 1 stitch before the gap, p2tog (one stitch from either side of the gap), turn.
Row 2 (RS): Slip 1 purlwise, knit to 1 stitch before the gap, ssk (one stitch from either side of the gap), turn.

Repeat these two rows until all gusset stitches have been worked [30 (32, 34) heel stitches].

leg
Resume working in the round.

Instep stitches: Continue working in pattern.
Heel stitches: Work in stockinette until you are on row 1 of pattern on front of leg. Thereafter work back of leg in the same manner as the front.

Repeat this round for approximately 4" or until leg is desired length, ending after chart row 19. Work two rounds in stockinette.

cuff
[K1, p1] repeat until cuff measures 1" / 2.5 cm. Bind off using Jeny's Amazingly Stretchy Bind-Off.

finishing
Weave in ends; block socks to desired measurements.

knit

 knit, wrapping yarn 3x around needle, this stitch will be slipped on subsequent rows until it is shown to knit it.

knit the slipped stitch from below

knit the slipped stitch from below, while at the same time wrapping yarn 3x around needle to create a new slipped stitch.

 wrap stitches. Slip 3 stitches with yarn in back, move yarn to front, slip the same 3 stitches back, move yarn to back and cinch.

 shows origin and destination of slipped stitch.

Chart 1

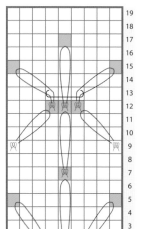

4. CLIO

sizes XS (S, M, L, XL, 2X, 3X, 4X, 5X) to fit bust measurements 28 (32, 36, 40, 44, 48, 52, 56, 60)". Sample shown is size M (36").

yarn Sport weight sock yarn, approximately 1070 (1110, 1150, 1200, 1250, 1300, 1350, 1400, 1450) yds (978 (1015, 1051, 1097, 1143, 1189, 1234, 1280, 1326)m) in main color, 305 (315, 325, 335, 345, 355, 365, 375, 385) yds (279 (288, 297, 306, 315, 324, 334, 343, 352)m) in contrast color.

Sample shown in Lorna's Laces Sportmate (70% superwash merino wool, 30% Outlast Viscose), 270 yds (247 m) per 100 g in color "Fjord" (main color) and "Natural" (contrast color).

needles US 4 (3.5 mm) circular needle, 32" or longer, or size needed to obtain gauge. You may want a second needle or double pointed needles of the same size for working sleeves (optional).

gauge 5.25 stitches / 8.75 rows per inch (2.5 cm) in stockinette worked flat.

notions Stitch markers, tapestry needle.

notes *This pattern is written with positive ease; choose the size that corresponds most closely to your ACTUAL bust circumference. To adjust the overall finished garment length, work more or fewer rows before beginning the back dart shaping. To adjust for petite or shorter-waisted proportions, shorten the work-even section between the back's decreases/increases, and work the increases every 4th row instead of every 6th row.*

lower body Using main color, cast on 150 (170, 190, 210, 230, 255, 280, 305, 330) stitches.

Row 1 (and all following WS rows): Purl all stitches.
RS Rows 2-10: K1, kfb, knit to last 3 stitches, kfb, k2 [10 stitches increased, all sizes].

Work these 160 (180, 200, 220, 240, 265, 290, 315, 340) stitches in stockinette (knit on RS, purl on WS rows) for 30 (30, 34, 34, 38, 38, 42, 44, 46) more rows.

shape back On next RS row, k58 (65, 73, 80, 88, 98, 108, 123, 133), k2tog, place marker, k80 (90, 100, 110, 120, 135, 150, 155, 170), place marker, ssk, k58 (65, 73, 80, 88, 98, 108, 123, 133) [2 stitches decreased, all sizes].

Work 3 rows in stockinette.

On next RS row, knit to 2 stitches before marker, k2tog, slip marker, knit to next marker, slip marker, ssk, knit to end. Repeat these 4 rows 3 times [8 stitches decreased (10 stitches total), all sizes].

Work 19 (19, 23, 23, 23, 25, 25, 25, 25) rows without shaping.

On the next RS row, knit to last stitch before marker, m1R, slip marker, knit to next marker, slip marker, m1L, knit to end. Work 5 rows stockinette. Repeat these 6 rows twice [total of 6 stitches increased, all sizes]. Remove markers.

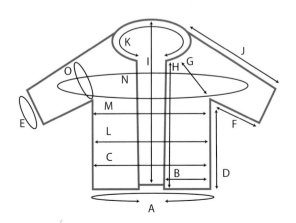

		XS (in)	S (in)	M (in)	L (in)	XL (in)	2X (in)	3X (in)	4X (in)	5X (in)
A	Hem circ	30.5	34.3	38.1	41.9	45.7	50.5	55.2	60.0	64.8
B	Front width	7.6	8.6	9.5	10.5	11.4	12.6	13.8	15.0	16.2
C	Back width	15.2	17.2	19.1	21.0	22.9	25.2	27.6	30.0	32.4
D	Side length (to underarm)	13.5	14.0	14.5	15.0	15.0	15.5	15.5	16.0	16.0
E	Wrist circ	9.5	10.3	11.0	11.8	12.6	13.3	14.1	14.1	14.1
F	Sleeve length (to underarm)	13.5	14.0	14.5	15.0	15.0	15.5	15.5	16.0	16.0
G	Yoke depth	4.9	5.6	5.6	6.6	6.6	6.7	7.2	7.2	7.7
H	Front length	16.1	16.9	17.6	18.1	18.3	18.8	18.8	19.5	19.5
I	Back length	20.1	21.5	22.3	24.0	24.3	24.9	25.3	26.0	26.5
J	Sleeve length (to neck)	19.4	20.9	21.6	23.1	23.3	24.0	24.4	25.1	25.6
K	Neck circ	21.0	21.0	22.1	22.1	22.9	24.6	25.5	25.7	25.9
L	Waist circ	28.6	32.4	36.2	40.0	43.8	48.6	53.3	58.1	62.9
M	Bust circ	29.7	33.5	37.3	41.1	45.0	49.7	54.5	59.2	64.0
N	Yoke circ	53.7	59.0	64.0	69.3	73.9	81.0	85.7	89.7	93.7
O	Upper arm	15.8	16.6	17.9	18.7	19.8	21.0	21.7	22.1	22.5

		XS (cm)	S (cm)	M (cm)	L (cm)	XL (cm)	2X (cm)	3X (cm)	4X (cm)	5X (cm)
A	Hem circ	77.4	87.1	96.8	106.4	116.1	128.2	140.3	152.4	164.5
B	Front width	19.4	21.8	24.2	26.6	29.0	32.1	35.1	38.1	41.1
C	Back width	38.7	43.6	48.4	53.2	58.1	64.1	70.2	76.2	82.3
D	Side length (to underarm)	34.3	35.6	36.8	38.1	38.1	39.4	39.4	40.6	40.6
E	Wrist circ	24.2	26.1	28.0	30.0	31.9	33.9	35.8	35.8	35.8
F	Sleeve length (to underarm)	34.3	35.6	36.8	38.1	38.1	39.4	39.4	40.6	40.6
G	Yoke depth	12.5	14.2	14.2	16.8	16.8	17.1	18.3	18.3	19.4
H	Front length	41.0	42.8	44.7	46.0	46.5	47.8	47.8	49.6	49.6
I	Back length	51.1	54.7	56.6	61.0	61.6	63.2	64.3	66.0	67.3
J	Sleeve length (to neck)	49.4	53.0	54.8	58.7	59.3	60.9	62.0	63.7	65.0
K	Neck circ	53.2	53.2	56.1	56.1	58.1	62.4	64.8	65.3	65.8
L	Waist circ	72.6	82.3	91.9	101.6	111.3	123.4	135.5	147.6	159.7
M	Bust circ	75.5	85.1	94.8	104.5	114.2	126.3	138.4	150.5	162.6
N	Yoke circ	136.4	150.0	162.6	176.1	187.7	205.6	217.7	227.9	238.0
O	Upper arm	40.2	42.1	45.5	47.4	50.3	53.2	55.1	56.1	57.1

Continue working these 156 (176, 196, 216, 236, 261, 286, 311, 336) stitches until work measures 13.5 (14, 14.5, 15, 15, 15.5, 15.5, 16, 16)" from cast-on edge.

bust shaping Optional bust shaping: if you have a smaller bust, you may opt not to work any shaping before joining the sleeves and working the yoke. If you have a fuller figure, consider adding horizontal bust darts in the front of the garment as follows for B (C, D)-cup shaping.

Right front dart: On next RS row, k40 (45, 50, 55, 60, 65, 70, 80, 85), wrap and turn, purl to end. Turn and k38 (43, 48, 53, 58, 63, 68, 78, 83), wrap and turn, purl to end. Repeat 2 (3, 4) times, wrapping and turning 2 stitches earlier each time. Turn and knit to end of row, picking up wraps and working them together with the wrapped stitches as you go.

Left front dart: With WS facing, p40 (45, 50, 55, 60, 65, 70, 80, 85), wrap and turn, knit to end. Turn and p38 (43, 48, 53, 58, 63, 68, 78, 83), wrap and turn, knit to end. Repeat 2 (3, 4) more times. Turn and purl to end of row, picking up wraps and working them together with the wrapped stitches as you go. Set work aside while you make the sleeves.

right sleeve Using main color and dpns (or a second set of circular needles, if you prefer the Magic Loop method) cast on 50 (54, 58, 62, 66, 70, 74, 74, 74) stitches. Join, being careful not to twist stitches, and work in the round for 3 rounds (knit all stitches). On next round, m1L, knit to end; knit 2 rounds.

Continue in this way, increasing 1 stitch at the beginning of every 3rd round, until you have 83 (87, 94, 98, 104, 110, 114, 116, 118) stitches. Work even until sleeve measures 13.5 (14, 14.5, 15, 15, 15.5, 15.5, 16, 16)" from cast-on edge. Place the first and last 5 (5, 6, 6, 7, 7, 8, 9, 10) stitches of the round (10 (10, 12, 12, 14, 14, 16, 18, 20) stitches total) on waste yarn or stitch holder. Break yarn, leaving about a 2' tail for seaming.

left sleeve Work as given for right sleeve, above, but with increases worked at the end of every third round as m1R. Place the 10 (10, 12, 12, 14, 14, 16, 18, 20) stitches at the beginning and end of the round on waste yarn or holder and break yarn, as for right sleeve.

join sleeves With RS of body facing, k35 (40, 44, 49, 53, 58, 62, 71, 75), place next 10 (10 12, 12, 14, 14, 16, 18, 20) stitches on waste yarn or holder, place marker, and knit all 73 (77, 82, 86, 90, 96, 98, 98, 98) stitches of the right sleeve, place marker, K66 (76, 84, 94, 102, 117, 130, 133, 146) stitches across the back, place next 10 (10 12, 12, 14, 14, 16, 18, 20) stitches on waste yarn or holder, place marker, and knit all 73 (77, 82, 86, 90, 96, 98, 98, 98) stitches of the left sleeve, place marker, K35 (40, 44, 49, 53, 58, 62, 71, 75) to end.

You should now have 282 (310, 336, 364, 388, 425, 450, 471, 492) stitches total.

Next row (WS): Purl all.

Next row (RS): [Knit to 2 sts before marker, k2tog, slip marker, ssk] four times; knit to end [8 sts decreased, all sizes].

Repeat these two rows 2 (3, 4, 4, 5, 5, 5, 6, 6) more times, 24 (32, 40, 40, 48, 48, 48, 56, 56) stitches decreased; 258 (278, 296, 324, 340, 377, 402, 415, 436) stitches remaining. Remove markers.

Work 3 more rows in stockinette without shaping (all sizes).

work yoke Set-up row: K22 (22, 23, 25, 27, 35, 38, 39, 42), cdd and mark this stitch. [K18 (20, 22, 24, 25, 27, 29, 30, 31), cdd and mark stitch] four times. K40 (44, 44, 52, 56, 61, 64, 67, 74) stitches across back, cdd and mark stitch. [K18 (20, 22, 24, 25, 27, 29, 30, 31), cdd and mark stitch] four times. K22 (22, 23, 25, 27, 32, 35, 36, 40) to end [20 stitches decreased, all sizes]. You should now have markers at ten points as shown in the diagram on next page. Work 5 rows stockinette.

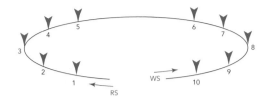

Decrease row (RS): [Knit to 1 stitch before marker, cdd and replace the marker at this stitch] repeat nine times; knit to end.

Work 5 rows stockinette, then another decrease row as given above (all sizes).

Short row for back shaping (always worked on the WS row immediately following a Decrease row): Purl to 5 stitches past marker #3, wrap and turn, knit to 5 stitches past marker #8, wrap and turn, purl to end.

Begin neckline shaping (all sizes): Starting with the next row (RS), work the first stitch and transfer it to a holder, then work as given across the remaining stitches. Continue to transfer the first stitch of each row from the needles to the holder in this fashion until you reach the end of the yoke; the number of live stitches will decrease by 1 on each row, and the number of stitches on the holders at each side should be the same at the end of WS rows.

Complete yoke shaping:

All sizes:

Rows 14-18: Stockinette.
Row 19: 4th Decrease row.

Size XS, S, M, L, XL only:

Rows 20-24: Stockinette.
Row 25: 5th decrease row.
Row 26: 2nd short row.
Rows 27-30: Stockinette.
Row 31: 6th decrease row.
Rows 32-36: Stockinette.
Row 37: 7th decrease row.
Row 38: 3rd short row.
Rows 39-42: Stockinette.

Size XS only:

Row 43: Work as for decrease row, but decrease only at markers 2, 4, 7, and 9 [110 stitches].

Continue to Finish Neck Edge section.

Size S only:

Row 43: K1 and transfer to holder, ssk, continue as for Decrease row to last 3 sts, k2tog, k1 (Markers 1 and 10 are removed).
Rows 44-48: Stockinette.
Row 49: Decrease only at markers 2, 4, 7, and 9 [112 stitches].

Continue to Finish Neck Edge section.

Size M only:

Row 43: 8th decrease row.
Rows 44-48: Stockinette.
Row 49: K1 and transfer to holder, cdd, continue as for decrease row to last 4 sts, cdd, k1 [118 stitches].

Continue to Finish Neck Edge section.

Size L only:

Row 43: 8th Decrease row.
Rows 44-48: Stockinette.
Row 49: Cdd and transfer to holder, continue as for decrease row to last 3 sts, cdd.
Row 50: 4th short row.
Rows 51-54: Stockinette.
Row 55: Repeat Row 49.
Rows 56-58: Stockinette.
Row 59: Decrease at markers 2, 4, 7, and 9 [120 stitches].

Continue to Finish Neck Edge section.

Size XL only:

Follow instructions for size L through row 58.

Row 59: Repeat Row 49 [126 stitches].

Continue to Finish Neck Edge section.

Sizes 2X–5X only:

Rows 20-24: Stockinette.
Row 25: 5th decrease row.
Rows 26-30: Stockinette.
Row 31: 6th decrease row.
Row 32: Short row.
Row 33-34: Stockinette.
Row 35: 7th decrease row.
Row 36-38: Stockinette.
Rows 39-54: Repeat rows 31-38 twice.
Rows 55-58: Repeat rows 31-34 once.

Size 2X only:

Row 59: Work as for decrease row, but decrease only at markers 2, 4, 7, and 9 [129 stitches].

Continue to Finish Neck Edge section.

Size 3X only:

Row 59: 13th decrease row.
Rows 60-62: Stockinette.
Row 63: Work as for decrease row, but decrease only at markers 2, 4, 7, and 9 [134 stitches].

Continue to Finish Neck Edge section.

Size 4X only:

Row 59-62: Repeat rows 35-38.
Row 63: 14th decrease row [135 stitches].

Continue to Finish Neck Edge section.

Size 5X only:

Row 59-66: Repeat rows 35-38 twice.
Row 67: 15th decrease row [136 stitches].

Continue to Finish Neck Edge section.

finish neck edge Turn and purl to end, including all of the held stitches at the right front. Turn and knit to end, including all of the held stitches at the left front. Purl all for a final row, then bind off knitwise on the RS and break yarn. There will be little gaps where the short-row stitches have been picked up from the holders, but this upper edge of the neckline will be underneath the lace edging and not visible in the finished garment.

Graft underarm openings closed using kitchener stitch and main color yarn, and weave in any loose ends. Place two markers on the bottom edge of the garment, directly under the center of the underarm sections, to mark the left and right sides. Block the body before proceeding; you will need to use the blocked garment as a reference when working the lace edging to fit.

Chart 1

Chart 3

Chart 2

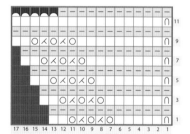

- ■ no stitch
- ☐ k on RS, p on WS
- ▬ p on RS, k on WS
- ⊼ k2tog
- ○ yo
- ⋂ slip stitch purlwise
- ◼ bind off

edging For cuffs (make 2 the same): Cast on 12 stitches in contrast color yarn, knit one row, then chart 1 to match sleeve hem circumference when lace is gently stretched, stopping at the end of a chart repeat. Bind off and break yarn.

For garment edging: Using contrast color yarn, cast on 12 stitches and knit one row. Follow chart 1 until work is about ¾" shorter than the distance from the side marker to the front edge when very gently stretched, being sure to stop at the end of a chart repeat.

Work [chart 2] 8 times to form the lower front corner (do not wrap the next stitch when turning for the short rows). Continue following the Sawtooth Lace Chart until this segment is about ¾" shorter than the front edge when gently stretched, again stopping at the end of a chart repeat. (For best results, lay the garment flat when measuring, and place the lace so that the knitted edge of the body fabric comes just to the edge of the eyelets in the lace.)

Work [chart 2] 8 times to form the upper front corner. Continue, now following chart 3 until the collar section fits the cast-off edge at the neckline. Work [chart 2] 8 times to form the second upper front corner. Work the same number of regular lace chart repeats for the second front edge segment, work the fourth corner to match the other three, and continue in the regular lace pattern until the final segment reaches around the lower front and back to meet the cast-on end of the lace trim. Bind off and break yarn.

finishing Pin lace in place along the cuffs and outside edge of the garment, using the corners, side markers, and center back neck as reference points, and matching up the cast-on and bound-off edges.

Using contrast color yarn and a tapestry needle, stitch the cast-on and bound-off edges together, then whip-stitch the garment edge to the lace, just above the eyelets. Check placement of the edging, pinning each of the points out straight if they tend to curl under. Next, still using contrast color yarn and tapestry needle, tack the inner edge of the lace in place on the garment at the peak and valley of each point. Gently steam finished garment, if desired, but do not press the lace edging.

5. TULIP DREAMS

sizes One size. Gauge and blocking will affect finished size.

yarn Fingering weight sock yarn, approximately 525 yds (480 m).

White shawl shown in Plymouth Yarn Dye for Me Happy Feet (90% superwash merino, 10% nylon), 480 yds (438 m) per 125 g in color "undyed," 2 skeins.

Pink shawl shown in handspun yarn.

needles US 5 (3.75 mm) circular needle 32" (81 cm) long, or size needed to obtain gauge.

US F (3.75 mm) crochet hook.

gauge 5 stitches / 9 rows per inch (2.5 cm) in stockinette, blocked.

notions 10 stitch markers, tapestry needle.

cast-on Using the cast-on method of your choice, cast on 3 stitches, knit 10 rows of garter stitch to form a small tab, do not turn. Pick up and knit 5 stitches down the side of the tab, pick up and knit 3 stitches on the bottom of the tab, turn [11 stitches].

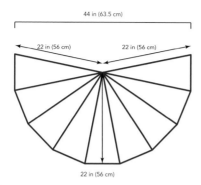

44 in (63.5 cm)

22 in (56 cm) 22 in (56 cm)

22 in (56 cm)

body

Row 1 (RS): K3, [kfb] twice, k1, [kfb] twice, k3 [15 stitches].

Row 2 (WS): K3, purl to last 3 stitches, k3.

Row 3: K3, place marker, [kfb, place marker] 9 times, k3 [24 stitches].

Row 4: K3, purl to last marker, k3.

Row 5: K3, slip marker, [kfb, knit to marker, slip marker] 9 times, k3.

Row 6: K3, purl to last marker, k3.

Row 7: Knit.

Row 8: K3, purl to last marker, k3.

Repeat rows 5-8 until there are 19 stitches between markers in each wedge, ending with row 8 [177 stitches].

border Work chart 1, knitting one full chart repeat in each wedge. At the same time, keep the 3 edge stitches at the beginning and end in garter stitch. When chart 1 is complete, you have 27 stitches per wedge and 6 edge stitches [249 stitches].

Work chart 2, knitting one full chart repeat in each wedge. At the same time, keep the 3 edge stitches at the beginning and end in garter stitch. Pay attention to the notes at the bottom of chart 2.

Work chart 3, knitting one full chart repeat in each wedge. At the same time, keep the 3 edge stitches at the beginning and end in garter stitch. Pay attention to the notes at the bottom of chart 3

When chart 3 is complete, you will have 36 stitches per wedge, 1 stitch after last repeat and 6 edge stitches [331 stitches]. Do not break

Chart 1

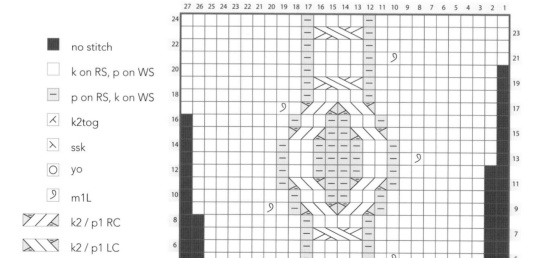

■	no stitch	
□	k on RS, p on WS	
▨	p on RS, k on WS	
◺	k2tog	
◹	ssk	
○	yo	
ꝯ	m1L	
▱	k2 / p1 RC	
▱	k2 / p1 LC	
▱	k2 / k2 LC	
▱	k2 / p1 / k2 LC	

yarn.

crochet bind-off With crochet hook, pick up first stitch on knitting needle, [chain 5, insert hook into the next 3 stitches and chain all 4 stitches together], repeat to end. Break yarn and pull through last loop.

finishing Weave in ends. Block on mat.

Chart 2

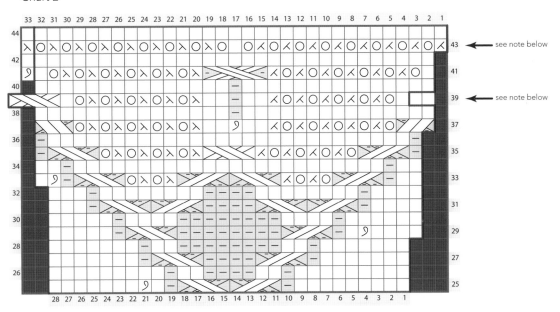

NOTE: *Repeat is within the red lines. On row 39 start as follows: k3 (garter edge), slip marker, k2 (first two stitches outside of repeat lines), continue with row 39 on chart. As you come to your markers, you will have to remove them before you do your k2 / k2 cable and replace them as follows: place two stitches on your cable needle and hold it in front, knit 2 stitches from your left hand needle, place marker, and knit your two stitches from your cable needle. Continue to repeat across the row as marked until 2 stitches before last marker, k2 slip marker, k3 (garter edging).*

*On row 43, **on the first repeat only** , replace the first k2tog with a knit. You will have to remove stitch markers (on all but the first repeat), by slipping the stitch before the marker, removing the marker, then slipping the stitch back to the left needle and placing the marker, then work k2tog (marker ends up before k2tog).*

Chart 3

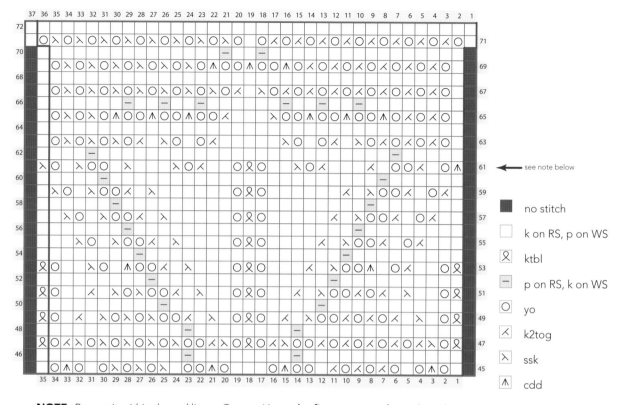

→ see note below

	no stitch
	k on RS, p on WS
⅄	ktbl
—	p on RS, k on WS
O	yo
∕	k2tog
∖	ssk
⋏	cdd

NOTE: *Repeat is within the red lines. On row 61, **on the first repeat only**, replace the leading cdd with a k2tog. For subsequent cdds you will have to remove each marker, work the cdd and replace it as you work through the row.*

6. POCKET PALS

sizes One size. Gauge and yarn choice will affect finished size.

yarn Fingering weight sock yarn, in small amounts.

Mouse – 21 yds main color; 0.5 yd black (for features).

Owl – 15.5 yds main color; 7 yds contrast color; 0.5 yd gold for beak.

Bunny – 17 yds main color, 1 yd white (for underside of tail), 0.5 yd black (for features).

Bluebird – 26 yds main color, 2 yds orange (for accent), 2 yds black (for beak, eyes, and feet).

Beaver – 17 yds main color, 2 yds contrast color for tail, 0.5 yd black (for features), 0.5 yd white for teeth.

needles US 1 / 2.25 mm or size needed to obtain gauge.

gauge 8 stitches / 10 rows per inch (2.5 cm) in stockinette. Note: It is more important to create a fabric that is firm and will not show stuffing than it is to meet a specific gauge.

notions Polyester fiberfill stuffing, tapestry needle, 4 buttons for owl's eyes (2 each size 7/16" and 2 each size 1/8" - felt discs may be substituted for buttons), sewing needle and buttonhole thread.

notes *For sewing on body pieces, embroidery, and "weaving in" ends, simply run the ends through the stuffing to an opposite side and clip. The wool and the stuffing should hold everything in place without tying knots.*

basic body Round begins and ends at center back.

Cast on 6 stitches. Join in a round.
Round 1: Kfb around [12 stitches].
Round 2: Knit.
Round 3: Kfb around [24 stitches].
Rounds 4-5: Knit.
Round 6: [Kfb, k1] repeat around [36 stitches].
Rounds 7-17: Knit.
Round 18: [K2tog, k8, ssk] repeat around [30 stitches].
Rounds 19-21: Knit.
Round 22: [K2tog, k6, ssk] repeat around [24 stitches].
Rounds 23-25: Knit.
Leaving stitches on the needles, stuff body.

Round 26: [K2tog, k4, ssk] repeat around [18 stitches].
Rounds 27-29: Knit.
Round 30: [K2tog, k2, ssk] repeat around [12 stitches].
Leaving stitches on the needles, stuff head.

Round 31: Knit.
Add stuffing to nose if needed.

Round 32: [K2tog, ssk] repeat around: 6 stitches.

mouse Complete basic body in main color. Break yarn and thread through remaining stitches, pull up, and weave in.

Tail: With main color, cast on 3 stitches. Work in 3-stitch I-cord until tail measures 3" (7.5 cm).

Ears (worked flat, make 2): With main color, cast on 5 stitches.
Row 1: P1, pfb, p1, pfb, p1 [7 stitches].
Row 2: Knit.
Row 3: Purl.
Row 4: Knit.
Row 5: P1, p2tog, p1, p2tog, p1 [5 stitches].
Row 6: Knit.
Row 7: P2tog, p1, p2tog [3 stitches].
Row 8: Cdd, bind off.
Repeat for second ear.

Assembly and finishing: Sew tail to back. Sew ears to sides of head as shown. With black, make duplicate stitch eyes and a satin stitch nose.

owl With main color, work basic body through round 17. Continue as follows:
Rounds 18-23: Knit.
Round 24: [K2tog, k8, ssk] repeat around [30 stitches].
Rounds 25-27: Knit.
Round 28: [K2tog, k6, ssk] repeat around [24 stitches].
Rounds 29-31: Knit.
Leaving stitches on the needles, stuff body.

Round 32: K2tog around [12 stitches].
Round 33: Knit.
Add stuffing if needed.

Round 34: K2tog around [6 stitches].
Break yarn and thread through remaining stitches, pull up, and weave in.

Wings, crown, and beak (worked flat):
With contrast color, cast on 4 stitches.
Row 1: Kfb across [8 stitches].
Row 2: Purl.
Row 3: Kfb across [16 stitches].
Row 4: Purl.
Row 5: Knit.
Row 6: Purl.
Row 7: [Kfb, k1] repeat around [24 stitches].
Row 8: P11, [pfb] twice, p11 [26 stitches].
Rows 9, 11, 13, 15, 17, and 19: Knit.
Rows 10, 12, 14, 16, 18 and 20: Purl.
Row 21: K1, ssk, k20, k2tog, k1[24 stitches].

Continue purling all wrong side rows.
Row 23: K1, ssk, k18, k2tog, k1 [22 stitches].
Row 25: K1, ssk, k6, ssk, k2tog, k6, k2tog, k1 [18 stitches].
Row 27: Ssk, k14, k2tog [16 stitches].
Row 29: Ssk, k12, k2tog [14 stitches].
Row 31: Ssk, k10, k2tog [12 stitches].
Row 33: Ssk, k8, k2tog [10 stitches].
Row 35: Ssk, k6, k2tog [8 stitches].
Row 37: Ssk, k4, k2tog [6 stitches].
Row 39: Ssk, k2, k2tog [4 stitches].
Break off contrast color; continue in gold for beak.

Row 41: K1, k2tog, k1 [3 stitches].
Row 43: Knit.
Row 45: Cdd, bind off.

Assembly and finishing: Sew wings, crown, and beak to body, beginning at cast on edges (bottom). Pinch folded corners of crown section into tufts and stitch in place. Sew end of beak in place. With sewing needle and buttonhole thread, securely sew buttons in place as shown, tying knots behind buttons before pushing through to back to clip off.

Safety note: Toys with buttons should not be available to small children who might choke on buttons if they work free. If the owl is intended for a small child, cut small discs of yellow felt or fleece fabric and secure them to the owl's face with black French knots for eyes.

bunny Complete basic body in main color.

Break yarn and thread through remaining stitches, pull up, and weave in.

Tail: With main color, cast on 5 stitches. Work 4 rows of 5-stitch I-cord in main color. Break yarn. Continue with 4 more rows of 5-stitch I-cord in white. Bind off.

Ears (worked flat, make 2): With main color, cast on 3 stitches.
Row 1 (and all WS rows): Purl.
Row 2: Kfb [twice], k1 [5 stitches].
Row 4: K1, kfb, k1, kfb, k1 [7 stitches].
Row 6: Knit.
Row 8: K1, ssk, k1, k2tog, k1 [5 stitches].
Row 10: Knit.
Row 12: Ssk, k1, k2tog [3 stitches].
Row 14: Cdd, bind off.
Repeat for second ear.

Assembly and finishing: Fold tail in half. Attach to back with white side down. Attach ears as shown. With black, make duplicate stitch eyes and a satin stitch nose.

beaver Complete basic body in main color. Break yarn and thread through remaining stitches, pull up, and weave in.

Tail (worked flat in garter stitch): With contrast color, cast on 5 stitches.

Row 1: Knit.
Row 2: K1, kfb, k1, kfb, k1 [7 stitches].
Row 3: Knit.
Row 4: K1, kfb, k3, kfb, k1 [9 stitches].
Rows 5-16: Knit.
Row 17: K1, ssk, k3, k2tog, k1 [7 stitches].
Rows 18-23: Knit.
Row 24: K1, ssk, k1, k2tog, k1 [5 stitches].
Rows 25-27: Knit.
Bind off.

Ears (make 2): With main color, cast on 2 stitches. Work in 2-stitch I-cord for five rows. Bind off. Repeat for second ear.

Assembly and finishing: Sew tail to back. Fold each ear in half and sew to crown as shown. With black, make duplicate stitch eyes and a satin stitch nose. With white, make two straight-stitch teeth on face, below nose.

bluebird With main color, complete basic body through round 6. Tail is shaped working flat over the 16 sts at center back. Continue as follows to shape tail:

Row 1: K8, turn.
Row 2: Slip 1, p8, p2tog, p1, turn.
Row 3: Slip 1, k3, ssk, k1, turn.
Row 4: Slip 1, p4, p2tog, p1, turn.
Row 5: Slip 1, k5, ssk, k1, turn.
Row 6: Slip 1, p6, p2tog, p1, turn.
Row 7: Slip 1, k7, ssk.

Complete knitting this current round as follows: k8, [kfb] 6 times, k12 [36 stitches]. Resume knitting basic body, completing rounds 7-32. Break yarn. Continue in black for beak.

Round 33 (with black): K2tog [three times] onto one needle. Continue in I-cord:
Row 1: K2tog, k1 [2 stitches].
Row 2: Knit.
Bind off. Weave in ends.

Wings (worked flat, make 2):
With main color, cast on 5 stitches.

Row 1 (and all WS rows): Purl .
Row 2: K1, kfb, k1, kfb, k1 [7 stitches].
Row 4: K2, kfb, k1, kfb, k2 [9 stitches].
Row 6: K3, kfb, k1, kfb, k3 [11 stitches].
Row 8: Knit.
Row 10: K3, ssk, k1, k2tog, k3 [9 stitches].
Rows 12 & 14: Knit.
Row 16: K2, ssk, k1, k2tog, k2 [7 stitches].
Row 18: K1, ssk, k1, k2tog, k1 [5 stitches].
Row 20: Ssk, k1, k2tog [3 stitches].
Row 22: Cdd, bind off.
Repeat for second wing.

Feet (make 2):
With black, cast on 2 stitches. Work in 2-stitch I-cord for five rows. Bind off. Repeat for second foot.

Assembly and finishing: Use duplicate stitch in orange to add accents on breast as shown. Sew wings to body as shown. Fold each foot in half and sew to body. With black, make duplicate stitch eyes. If desired, stuff a bit of stuffing behind the top of each wing where it is sewn to body.

7. DEVONIAN

sizes One size. To change sizes, go up or down in needle/yarn gauge.

yarn Fingering weight sock yarn, approximately 400 yds (366 m).

Sample shown in String Theory Caper Sock (80% superwash merino wool, 10% cashmere, 10% nylon), 400 yds (366 m) per 113 g in color "Avalon."

needles US 1 (2.25 mm) dpns or circular needle, or size needed to obtain gauge.

gauge 9 stitches / 12.5 rows per inch (2.5 cm) in stockinette worked in the round.

notions Stitch markers, tapestry needle.

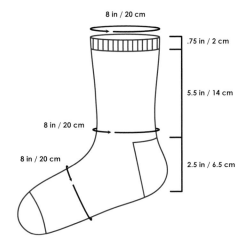

cast-on Cast on 24 stitches using Judy's magic cast-on (12 heel stitches, 12 instep stitches). Knit one round.

toe

Round 1:
Heel stitches: k1, Rli, knit until 1 stitch remains, Lli, k1.
Instep stitches: Repeat sole stitches.

Round 2: Knit.

Repeat rounds 1 and 2 until there are 60 stitches [30 instep stitches, 30 sole stitches].

foot Work in stockinette on both instep and sole stitches until sock measures 5 inches / 12.75 cm less than total foot measurement.

gusset

Set-up round:
Heel stitches: Knit.
Instep stitches: K14, place marker, k2, place marker, k14.

Next round:
Heel stitches: Knit.
Instep stitches: Work to marker, slip marker, work following chart 1, slip marker, work to end of instep stitches.

Work this last round until chart 1 is complete. You will be increasing every other round on the instep stitches according to the chart.

heel turn The heel turn is worked over the sole stitches only.

K1, Lli, k1, [slip 1, k1] until 2 stitches before end of sole, wrap and turn [31 stitches]. Purl to 2 stitches before end of sole, wrap and turn.

Row 1: [K1, slip 1], repeat until stitch before previous wrap, wrap and turn.
Row 2: Purl to stitch before wrapped st, wrap and turn.
Row 3: [Slip 1, k1], repeat until stitch before previous wrap, wrap and turn.
Row 4: Purl to stitch before wrapped st, wrap and turn.

Repeat rows 1-4 until there are 20 wrapped stitches and 9 stitches between them [1 unwrapped +10 wrapped +9 middle +10 wrapped +1 unwrapped = 31 heel stitches].

Next row: [K1, slip 1] repeat across until you reach the first wrapped stitch. Lift and knit wraps (k2tog-tbl) until last wrap, k3tog-tbl with final stitch, turn.

Slip 1, purl across, lift and purl wraps until last wrap, p3tog with final stitch, turn [29 heel stitches].

heel flap

Row 1: [Slip 1, k1] across. Work last stitch and first gusset stitch together with ssk.
Row 2: Slip 1, purl across. Work last stitch and first gusset stitch together with p2tog.

Repeat rows 1 and 2 until all of the gusset stitches are used [72 total stitches].

leg transition Slip one, knit 14. Rearrange stitches comfortably so this is now the start of your round. Remove markers if desired.

Work following chart 2 until chart is complete.

leg Work following chart 3 until chart is complete.

cuff Work following chart 4 until chart is complete. Work 8 more rounds of p1, k1 ribbing as established. Bind off using Jeny's Surprisingly Stretchy Bind-Off.

finishing Weave in ends; block socks to desired measurements.

Chart 1

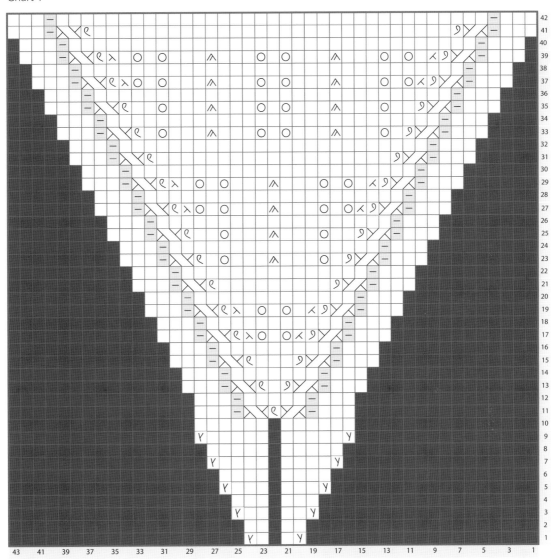

⬛ no stitch	Ｙ Rli	⌐ m1R
⬜ k on RS, p on WS	Ｙ Lli	ℓ m1L
− p on RS, k on WS	⋏ slip 1, k2tog, psso	⋉ k1 / k1 RC
⋋ k2tog	⋒ pass stitch over (see notes)	⋈ k1 / k1 LC
⋌ ssk	O yo	⋉⋋ k1 / k1 RC with k2tog
⋋ p2tog		

Chart 2

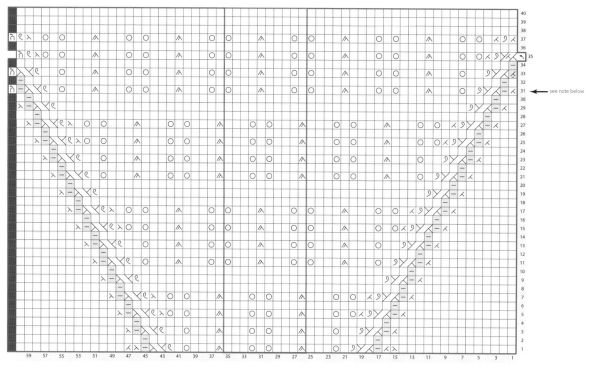

NOTE: *Work the stitches within the red box a total of two times before moving on in the chart. On row 31 of chart 2, you have the first instance of the special slip/pass over symbol. Work the round according to the chart. At the end of the round, slip the last stitch of the round and pass it over the first stitch of the round, which was a k2tog, creating a sk2p right at the beginning/end of the round. Do this for all subsequent instances of this symbol.*

Chart 3

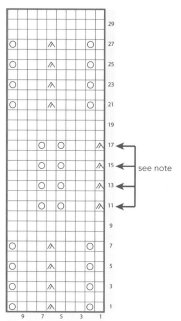

NOTE: *On rounds 11, 13, 15 and 17, of chart 3 and rounds 1, 3, 5 and 7 of chart 4; work the first instance of the sk2p using the special slip/pass over technique, i.e. slip the last stitch of the round and pass it over the first stitch of the round, which was a k2tog, creating a sk2p right at the beginning/end of the round.*

Chart 4

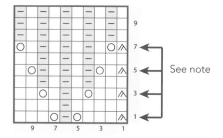

8. SEMADAR

sizes Small (medium, large).

yarn Fingering weight sock yarn, approximately 385-425 yds (347-388 m).

Sample shown in Girl on the Rocks BFL sock yarn (80% superwash bluefaced leicester wool, 20% nylon), 425 yds (388 m) per 100 g in color "Iron Oxide."

needles US 1 (2.25 mm) dpns or circular needle, or size needed to obtain gauge.

Dpns or circular needle one size smaller than main needle(s).

gauge 9 stitches / 13 rows per inch (2.5 cm) in stockinette worked in the round.

notions Tapestry needle.

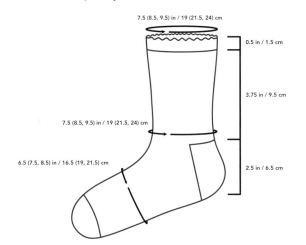

cast-on Cast on 56 (64, 72) stitches using a provisional cast-on; join in the round without twisting.
Work [p1, k1] ribbing for 5 rounds. [K2tog, yo], repeat to end of round. Knit 5 rounds.

Remove provisional cast-on, placing live stitches on smaller needle(s). Fold provisional edge to inside of cuff. Knit together 1 stitch from working needle with corresponding stitch from smaller needle, until all the stitches have been joined together. Knit one round plain.

leg Work following chart 1 rounds 1-16. You have 7 (8, 9) repeats of the chart around circumference. When chart 1 is complete, repeat [chart 1] 2 (3, 3) more times, or until desired leg length.

heel NOTES: *Heel is worked over 28 (32, 36) stitches. For size small and large only, knit 4 more stitches before beginning heel. This will center the lace repeat for the foot.*

Row 1 (WS): K3, p22 (26, 30), k3
Row 2 (RS): K3, [k1, slip 1] repeat to last 3 stitches, k3.
Row 3: K3, p22 (26, 30), k3.
Row 4: K3, [slip 1, k1] repeat to last 3 stitches, k3.
Repeat [rows 1-4] 6 (7, 8) more times, 28 (32, 36) rows total. End having completed a RS row.

heel turn
Row 1 (WS): Slip 1, p15 (17, 19), p2tog, p1, turn.
Row 2 (RS): Slip 1, k5, ssk, k1, turn.
Row 3: Slip 1, p6, p2tog, p1, turn.
Row 4: Slip 1, k7, ssk, k1, turn.
Row 3: Slip 1, p8, p2tog, p1, turn.

Continue working in this manner, working 1 more stitch before the decrease on each successive row until all stitches have been worked. End having completed a WS row, turn.

Slip 1, knit across.

gusset Pick up and knit 14 (16, 18) sts along the side of the heel flap for right gusset. Work across instep stitches, following first row of chart 2 small (medium, large), increase 1 stitch. Pick up and knit 14 (16, 18) stitches along the side of the heel flap for left gusset [85 (97, 109) stitches]. Knit to end of heel stitches, including gusset stitches.

Round 1
Instep stitches: Work following chart 2.
Heel stitches: Knit.

Round 2
Instep stitches: Work following chart 2.
Heel stitches: k1, ssk, knit to 3 stitches before end of heel stitches, k2tog, k1.

Repeat rounds 1 and 2 until you have 28 (32, 36) heel stitches [57 (65, 73) stitches].

foot
instep stitches: Work following chart 2 small (medium, large).
heel stitches: Knit.

Chart 1 all sizes

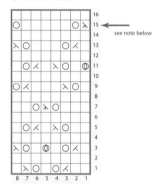

see note below

NOTE: On row 15 of chart, at beginning of round only, the sssk will combine the last stitch of the previous round with the first two stitches of this round.

Chart 2 (medium)

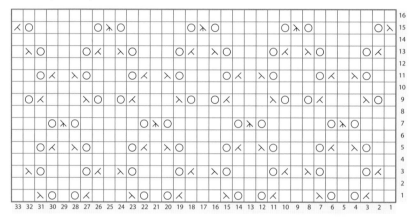

Chart 2 (small, large)

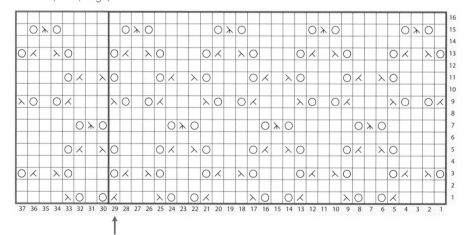

	k on RS, p on WS
⊼	k2tog
⋋	ssk
人	sssk
O	yo
⓪	nupp

NOTE: for size small work only the stitches within the red box. At stitch 29 on the first row only, work a knit stitch instead of k2tog. For size large, work all stitches. Work stitch 29 as charted.

Continue in this manner until foot measures 2″ less than desired length. End with a plain knit row before beginning the next section.

toe Work across remaining heel stitches so that new round will begin at instep stitches.

Round 1
Instep stitches: K1, ssk, knit to 3 stitches before end of instep stitches, k2tog, k1.
Heel stitches: Repeat instep stitches.

Round 2
Instep stitches: Knit.
Heel stitches: Knit.

Repeat these two rounds until 15 (17, 19) sts remain. Decrease one more stitch on instep stitches so that you have an even number of stitches.

finishing Close toe with Kitchener stitch; weave in ends.

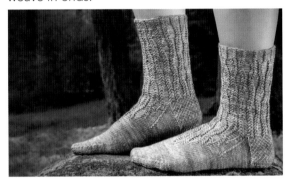

9. CAMBIUM

sizes Small (medium, large). Shown in size medium.

yarn Fingering weight sock yarn, approximately 395 yds (361 m).

Sample shown in Madeline Tosh Tosh Sock (100% superwash merino wool), 395 yds (361 m) per 114 g in color "Earl Grey."

needles US 1 (2.25 mm) dpns or circular needle, or size needed to obtain gauge.

gauge 8 stitches / 11.5 rows per inch (2.5 cm) in stockinette worked in the round.

notions Stitch markers, tapestry needle.

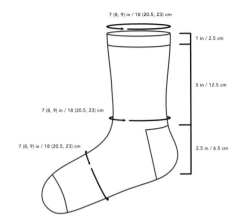

cast-on Cast on 56 (64, 72) stitches using the cast-on of your choice; join in the round without twisting.

cuff
Right Sock:
Round 1: [K2, p2] to end of round.
Round 2: [RT, p2] to end of round.

Repeat these two rounds until the cuff measures 1.5″ / 4 cm, ending after round 2.

Left Sock:
Round 1: [P2, k2] to end of round.
Round 2: [P2, LT] to end of round.

Repeat these two rounds until the cuff measures 1.5″ / 4 cm, ending after round 2. The rest of the instructions refer to both left and right socks.

leg Work rows 1-24 of Chart 1 until leg measures 6″ / 15 cm or desired length, ending after either row 12 or row 24.

heel If you just finished working row 12, k6 (4, 6) and turn work to start heel flap. If you just finished working row 24, k2 (0, 2) and turn work to start heel flap.

Heel is worked back and forth over the 28 (32, 36) stitches facing you (WS). Set the remaining stitches aside on a stitch holder or spare needle until you start working the top of the foot.

Row 2: [Slip 1, k1] 14 (16, 18) times.
Row 3: Repeat row 1.
Row 4: [K1, slip 1] 13 (15, 17) times, k2.

Repeat these four rows until heel flap measures 2.25" / 5.5 cm or desired length. For higher insteps, knit a longer heel flap. For lower insteps, knit a shorter heel flap. End after a WS row.

heel turn

Row 1 (RS): Slip 1, k16 (18, 20), ssk, k1, turn.
Row 2: Slip 1, p7, p2tog, p1, turn.
Row 3: Slip 1, knit to 1 stitch before gap created by turn on previous row, ssk, k1, turn.
Row 4: Slip 1, purl to 1 stitch before gap created by turn on previous row, p2tog, p1, turn.

Repeat rows 3 and 4 until all stitches have been worked [18 (20, 22) stitches].

gusset
Slip 1, k8 (9, 10), place marker to mark beginning of round, k9 (10, 11) remaining heel stitches.

Knit into each selvedge stitch along right edge of heel flap, M1 between heel flap and top of foot, place marker for right side of instep. Work row 1 of Chart 2 (for the appropriate size) across held instep stitches, place marker for left side of instep. M1 between top of foot and heel flap, knit into each selvedge stitch along left edge of heel flap. Knit to end of round marker. Redistribute stitches as desired across needles.

Round 1: Knit to 2 stitches before right instep marker, k2tog, slip marker, work next row of

Chart 1

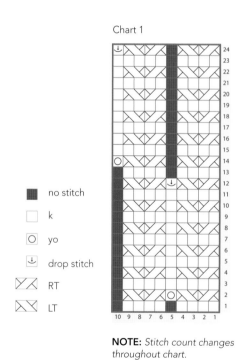

no stitch

☐ k

Ⓞ yo

↧ drop stitch

⧗ RT

⧗ LT

NOTE: *Stitch count changes throughout chart.*

Chart2 (Small)

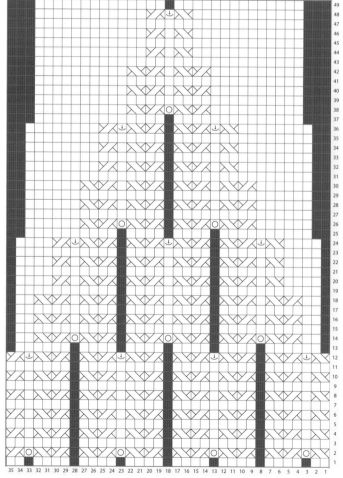

Chart 2 across instep, slip marker, ssk, knit to end of round.

Round 2: Knit to marker, slip marker, work next row of Chart 2 across instep, slip marker, knit to end of round.

Repeat these two rounds until 28 (32, 36) sole stitches remain [56 (64, 72) stitches total].

foot Repeat round 2 from gusset section (above) until sock measures 1.75 (2, 2.5)" / 4.5 (5, 6.5) cm less than desired length. After you've worked all rows of Chart 2 once, continue working the last row of Chart 2 (knit every stitch).

toe Remove beginning of round marker. Knit to right side of foot marker; this is now also the beginning of the round.

Round 1: [Slip marker, k1, ssk, knit to 3 stitches before marker, k2tog, k1] repeat to end.

Round 2: Knit around, slipping markers as you come to them.

Repeat these two rounds until 16 stitches remain.

Chart 2 (Medium)

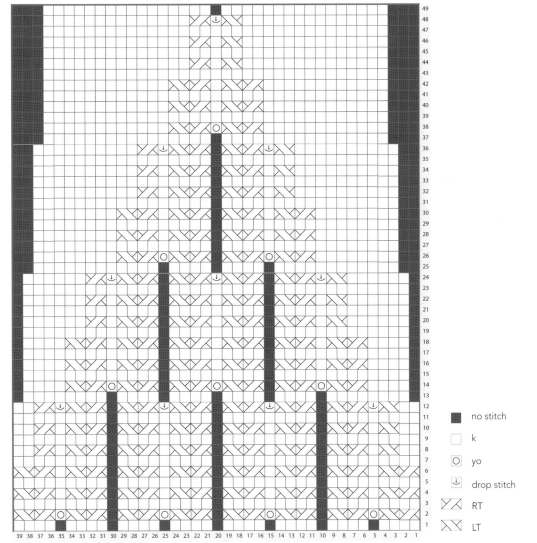

finishing Close toe with Kitchener stitch; weave in ends.

Chart2 (Large)

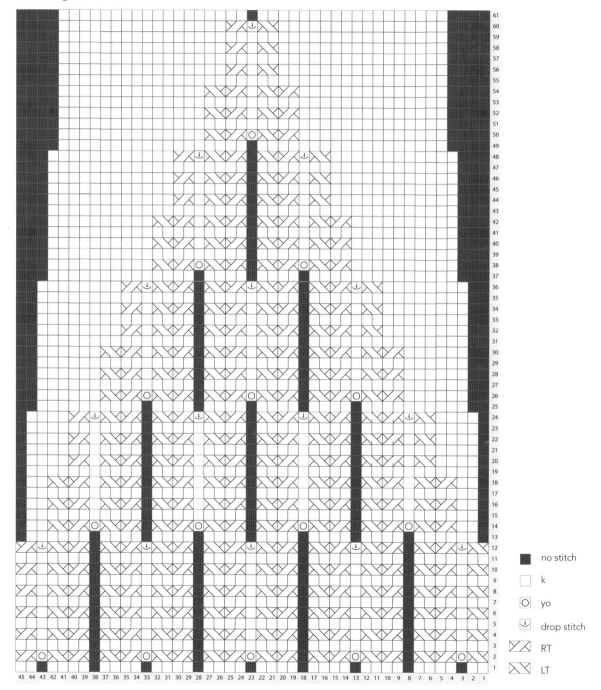

■	no stitch
□	k
Ⓞ	yo
↓	drop stitch
⤫	RT
⤬	LT

10. WANDERLUST

sizes Small (large).

yarn Fingering weight sock yarn, approximately 345 (382) yds (315 (349) m) main color and 115 (134) yds (105 (122) m) contrast color.

Sample shown in Regia Die Sockenwolle (75% wool, 25% nylon), 230 yds (210 m) per 50 g in colors "02006 mineral blue" (main color), 2 skeins and "06770 night blue" (contrast color), 1 skein.

needles US 1 (2.25 mm) dpns or circular needle, or size needed to obtain gauge.

gauge 8 stitches / 11.5 rows per inch (2.5 cm) in stockinette worked in the round.

notions Tapestry needle.

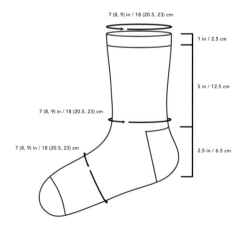

cast-on Cast on 60 (68) stitches in contrast color using the cast-on of your choice, join in the round without twisting.

cuff Knit 5 rounds stockinette in contrast color. Cut contrast color yarn, switch to main color and knit one round. Work 21 rounds [k1, p1] ribbing in main color. Work 1 round stockinette, increasing by 4 stitches evenly spaced apart [64 (72) stitches].

leg Work following chart 1 small (large) LEFT or RIGHT.

heel **NOTE:** *The heel begins with knit stitches for the right sock (first half of stitches), and purl stitches for the left sock (last half of stitches). Heels are worked in a double strand of the main color.*

Right sock:

NOTE: *On first knit row only, decrease by 4 stitches evenly spaced [28 (32) stitches]. To avoid holes, begin the last purl row and the first knit row of the right foot with a yo. In the next round of the foot, this yo will be knitted together with the first and last stitches of the instep stitches.*

Row 1: Knit until one heel stitch remains, slip last stitch to instep needle, turn.
Row 2: Purl until one heel stitch remains, slip last stitch to instep needle, turn.

Repeat rows 1 and 2 until you have 10 (12) heel stitches remaining.

Row 1: Knit to end of heel stitches, slip 1 from instep needle onto heel needle. Knit stitch directly below slipped stitch. Pass the slipped stitch over the stitch you just knit. Wrap next stitch, turn.
Row 2: Purl to end of heel stitches, slip 1 from instep needle onto heel needle. Purl stitch directly below slipped stitch. Pass the slipped stitch over the stitch you just purled. Wrap next stitch, turn.

Repeat rows 1 and 2 until you have 28 (32) heel stitches.

Left Sock:

NOTE: *On first purl row only, decrease by 4 stitches evenly spaced [28 (32) stitches]. To avoid holes begin the first purl row and the last knit row of the left heel with a yo. In the first round of the foot this yo will be knitted together with the first and last stitches of the instep stitches.*

Row 1: Purl until one heel stitch remains, slip last stitch to instep needle, turn.

Row 2: Knit until one heel stitch remains, slip last stitch to instep needle, turn.

Repeat rows 1 and 2 until you have 10 (12) heel stitches remaining.

Row 1: Purl to end of heel stitches; slip 1 from instep needle onto heel needle. Purl stitch directly below slipped stitch. Pass the slipped stitch over the stitch you just knit. Wrap next stitch, turn.

Row 2: Knit to end of heel stitches, slip 1 from

Chart 1 small RIGHT

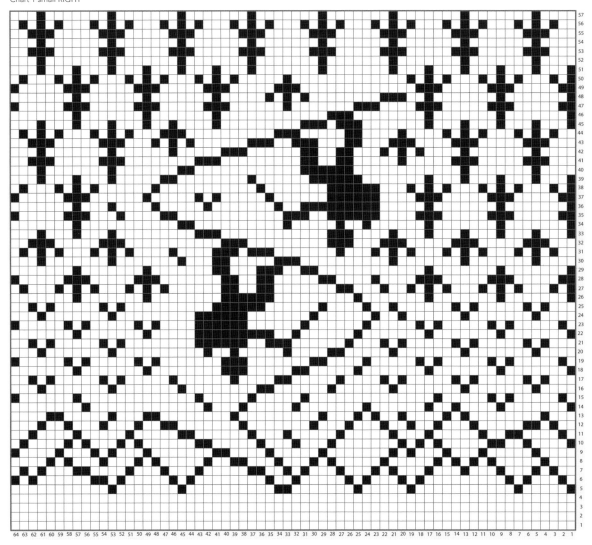

 main color contrast color

instep needle onto heel needle. Knit stitch directly below slipped stitch. Pass the slipped stitch over the stitch you just purled. Wrap next stitch, turn.

Repeat rows 1 and 2 until you have 28 (32) heel stitches.

foot NOTE: *Row 1 of chart 2 has four increase points. To increase at these points, knit once into one strand of the double stranded heel stitch, and once into the other strand, creating* *two stitches from one.*

Work following chart 2 small (large) until sock measures 2 inches less than overall length.

toe Knit one round in main color. Add second strand in main color and knit one round. Thereafter work with 2 strands of main color.

Note: *To avoid bumpy decreases, decreased stitches are worked with only one strand.*

Chart 1 small LEFT

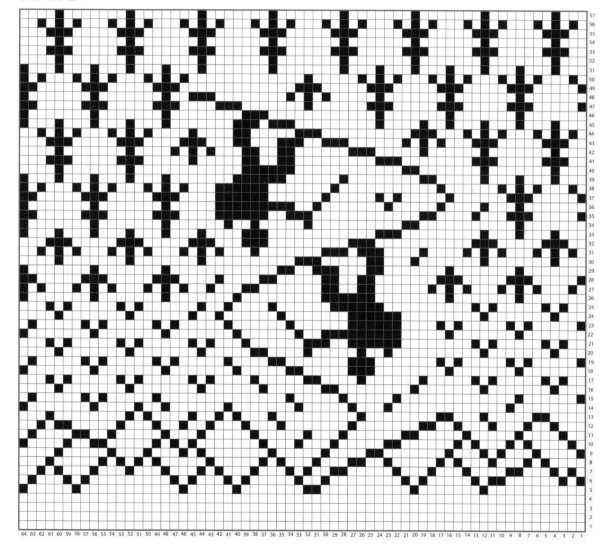

Round 1:

Instep stitches: K1 with two strands, k2 with one strand only, knit with two strands until 3 stitches remain, k2 with one strand only, k1 with two strands.

Heel stitches: Repeat instep stitches.

Round 2 (entire round with two strands):

Instep stitches: K1 with two strands, ssk, work until 3 stitches remain, k2tog, k1.

Heel stitches: Repeat instep stitches.

Repeat rounds 1 and 2. Repeat round 1 once more.

Round 3:

Instep stitches: K1 with 2 strands, ssk with one strand, k1 with 1 strand, knit with two strands until 4 stitches remain, k1 with 1 strand, k2tog with one strand, k1 with 2 strands.

Heel stitches: repeat instep stitches.

Repeat round 3 until 12 stitches remain.

Round 4 (work entire round with one strand):

[K1, k2tog, ssk, k1], repeat.

finishing Break yarn and thread through tapestry needle. Thread needle through the 8 live stitches and cinch tightly. Weave in ends.

Chart 1 (large) RIGHT

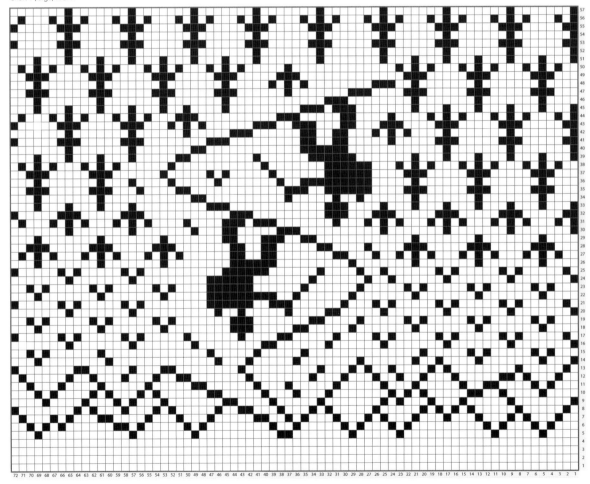

Chart 1 large LEFT

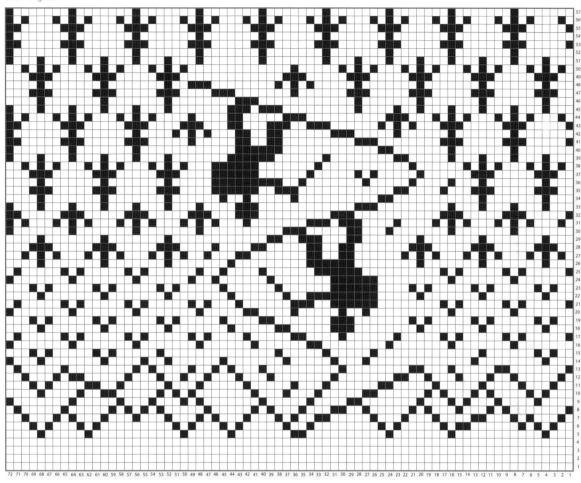

■ contrast color □ main color

Chart 2 (small)

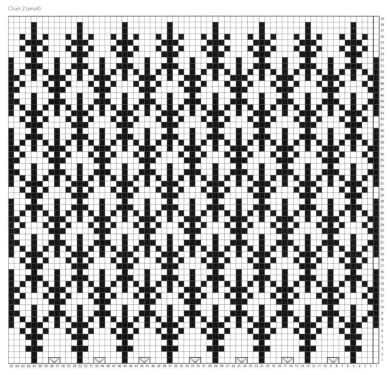

NOTE: For RIGHT sock work chart including stitches in red and purple boxes and excluding stitches in blue boxes.
For LEFT sock work chart including stitches in blue and purple boxes and excluding stitches in red boxes.

Chart 2 (large)

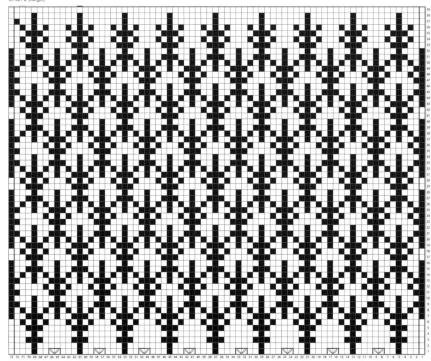

11. PHAEODARIA

sizes Small (medium, large).

yarn Fingering weight sock yarn, approximately 300-375 yds (292-342 m).

Sample shown in Sweet Georgia Yarns CashLuxe Fine (70% superwash merino wool, 20% cashmere, 10%nylon), 375 yds (342 m) per 115 g in color "Ginger."

needles US 1 (2.25 mm) dpns or circular needle, or size needed to obtain gauge.

gauge 9 stitches / 12 rows per inch (2.54 cm) in stockinette worked in the round.

notions Cable needle (optional), tapestry needle.

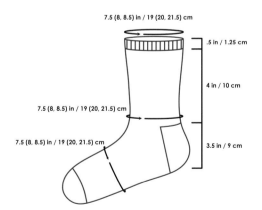

7.5 (8, 8.5) in / 19 (20, 21.5) cm
.5 in / 1.25 cm
4 in / 10 cm
7.5 (8, 8.5) in / 19 (20, 21.5) cm
7.5 (8, 8.5) in / 19 (20, 21.5) cm
3.5 in / 9 cm

cast-on Using your favorite cast on method, cast on 66 (72, 78) stitches. Join in the round taking care not to twist your stitches. Divide into two sets of stitches, 33 (37, 39) instep stitches and 33 (35, 39) heel stitches.

leg NOTE: *On charts 1 and 2: for size small, work stitches 2-12 only; for size medium, work stitches 1-12 only. For size large, work all stitches.*

Work following chart 1 until chart is complete.

Work following chart 2. When chart 2 is complete, repeat chart until leg reaches 4 inches or desired height. End having completed row 6 of chart 2.

heel NOTE: *Heel is worked over stitches 36-66 (38-72, 40-78). Heel flap is 33 (35, 39) stitches.*

Row 1 (WS): Work following chart 3.
Row 2 (RS): Work following chart 3 small (medium, large).
Repeat rows 1-2 16 (17, 19) more times, 32 (36, 40) rows total. End having completed a RS row.

heel turn
Row 1 (WS): Slip 1, p17 (19, 21), p2tog, p1, turn.
Row 2 (RS): Slip 1, k4 (6, 6), ssk, k1, turn.
Row 3: Slip 1, p5 (7, 7), p2tog, p1, turn.
Row 4: Slip 1, k6 (8, 8), ssk, k1, turn.
Row 5: Slip 1, p7 (9, 9), p2tog, p1, turn.

Continue working in this manner, working 1 more stitch before the decrease on each successive row, until all stitches have been worked. End having completed a RS row [19 (21, 23) stitches].

gusset Pick up and knit 16 (18, 20) sts along the side of the heel flap for right gusset.

Work across instep stitches, following first row of chart 2 (**NOTE:** *for size medium only there will be one extra stitch not covered by the chart. Purl it*). Pick up and knit 16 (18, 20) stitches along the side of the heel flap for left gusset. Knit to end of heel stitches (including gusset stitches).

Chart 1

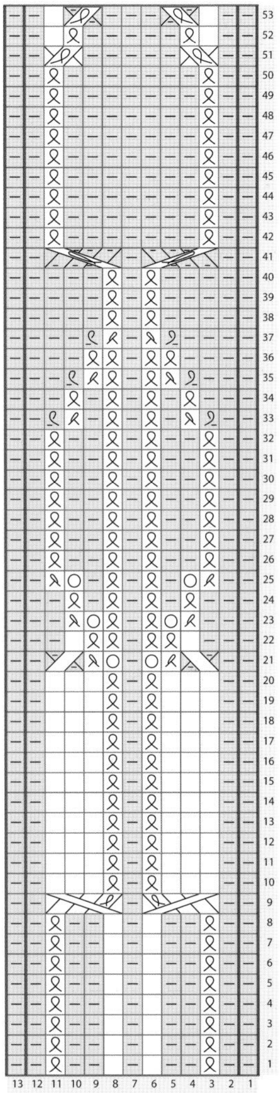

- k on RS, p on WS
- p on RS, k on WS
- slip purlwise
- k tbl
- k2tog tbl
- ssk tbl
- yo
- m1L purlwise
- m1R purlwise
- k1tbl / k1 RC
- k1tbl / k1 LC
- k1 / p1 RC
- k1 / p1 LC
- k1 tbl / p1 RC
- k1 tbl / p1 LC
- k1 tbl / p3 RC
- k1 tbl / p3 LC
- k1 / k2 k1 tbl RC
- k1 / k2 k1 tbl LC
- k1 tbl / p1 / k1 tbl RC

NOTE: *On both chart 1 and chart 2; for size small work stitches 2-12 (center area between red and blue) only for size medium work stitches 1-12 (include stitches between red lines) only, for size large work all stitches (include stitches between red lines and stitches between blue lines).*

Special Instructions:

On the RIGHT SOCK, slip 2 to cable needle, hold in back, k 1through the back loop. Slip the 2 stitches on the cable needle back to the left needle. slip 1 to cable needle, hold in front, purl 1, knit 1 through the back loop from cable needle.

On the LEFT SOCK, slip 2 to cable needle, hold in front, k 1through the back loop. Slip the 2 stitches on the cable needle back to the left needle. slip 1 to cable needle, hold in front, purl 1, knit 1 through the back loop from cable needle.

Chart 2

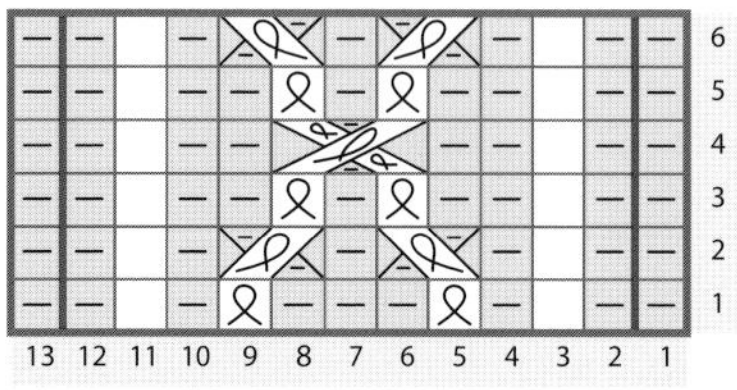

Chart 3 Small

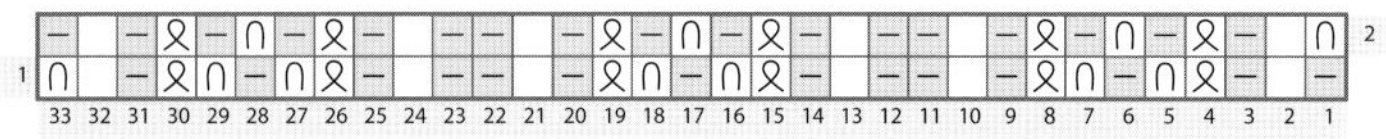

Chart 3 Medium

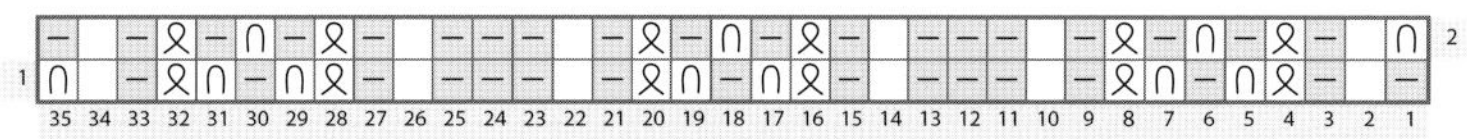

Chart 3 Large

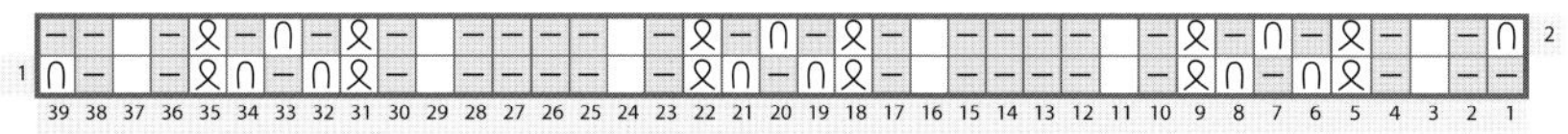

- k on RS, p on WS
- p on RS, k on WS
- ktbl on RS, ptbl on WS
- slip purlwise

Round 1

Instep stitches: Work following chart 2.
Heel stitches: Knit.

Round 2

Instep stitches: Work following chart 2.
Heel stitches: K1, ssk, knit to 3 stitches before end of heel stitches, k2tog, k1.

Repeat rounds 1 and 2 until you have 33 (35, 39) heel stitches [66 (74, 78) stitches].

foot

Instep stitches: Work following chart 2 small (medium, large).
Heel stitches: Knit.

Continue in this manner until foot measures 2.5 (2.25, 2)" less than desired length. End having completed row 6 of chart 2.

toe
Work across remaining heel stitches so that new round will begin at instep stitches.

Round 1

Instep stitches: K1, ssk, work in ribbing pattern as established to 3 stitches before end of instep stitches, k2tog, k1.
Heel stitches: K1, ssk, knit to 3 stitches before end of heel stitches, k2tog, k1.

Round 2

Instep stitches: K2, work in ribbing pattern as established to 2 stitches before end of instep stitches, k2.
Heel stitches: Knit.

Repeat these two rounds 5 (7, 8) more times, [42 stitches]. Work [round 1] 6 more times [18 stitches].

finishing
Close toe with Kitchener stitch. Weave in ends.

12. ARCADIA

sizes One size. Gauge and blocking will affect finished size.

yarn Fingering weight sock yarn, approximately 460 yds (420 m).

Red sample shown in Hazel Knits Entice (70% superwash merino wool, 20% cashmere, 10% nylon) 400 yds (366 m) per 115 g, 2 skeins, in color "Ruby Love."

Grey sample shown in Abstract Fibers Mighty Sock (50% Merino, 50% Tencel) 380 yds (347 m) per 115 g, 2 skeins in color "Silver."

needles US 5 (3.75 mm) or size needed to obtain gauge.

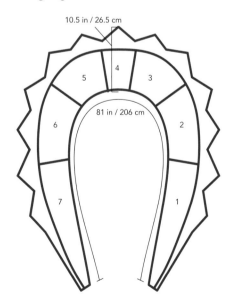

12. ARCADIA

sizes One size. Gauge and blocking will affect finished size.

yarn Fingering weight sock yarn, approximately 460 yds (420 m).

Red sample shown in Hazel Knits Entice (70% superwash merino wool, 20% cashmere, 10% nylon) 400 yds (366 m) per 115 g, 2 skeins, in color "Ruby Love."

Grey sample shown in Abstract Fibers Mighty Sock (50% Merino, 50% Tencel) 380 yds (347 m) per 115 g, 2 skeins in color "Silver."

needles US 5 (3.75 mm) or size needed to obtain gauge.

gauge 6.5 stitches / 8 rows per inch (2.5 cm) in garter stitch after blocking.

notions Tapestry needle.

cast-on Using your favorite cast-on method, cast on 3 stitches.

body Work the body of the shawl in garter stitch. Every RS row begins with a yarn over; this will leave loops on one edge of the shawl. When you are working the RS of the shawl, the loops will be on the right-hand edge. This is where you will later pick up stitches for the lace border. The body of the shawl is worked in sections as shown on the schematic.

Section 1 - Tail Wing A (144 rows, 72 loops)

Row 1: Knit
Row 2: Yo, k2tog, knit to end of row.
Row 3: Knit
Row 4: Yo, k2tog, knit to end of row.
Row 5: Knit
Row 6: Yo, k2tog, knit to end of row.
Row 7: Knit.
Row 8 (increase row): Yo, knit to end of row.

Repeat rows 1-8 until you have increased 18 times [21 stitches]. End having completed an increase row.

Section 2 - Short Row Wedge 1A (72 rows, 36 loops)

NOTE: *In this section, and all subsequent sections, any time you encounter a wrapped stitch made on a previous row, pick up the wrap and knit it together with the wrapped stitch.*

Row 1: Knit.
Row 2: Yo, k2tog, knit until 3 stitches remain, wrap and turn.
Row 3: Knit.
Row 4: Yo, k2tog, knit to end of row.
Row 5: Knit.
Row 6: Yo, k2tog, knit to end of row.
Row 7: Knit.
Row 8 (increase row): Yo, knit to end of row.

Repeat short row wedge 1A 8 more times (9 repeats total) [30 stitches].

Section 3 - Short Row Wedge 2A (60 rows, 30 loops)

Row 1: Knit.
Row 2: Yo, k2tog, knit until 11 stitches remain, wrap and turn.
Row 3: Knit.
Row 4: Yo, k2tog, knit until 7 stitches remain, wrap and turn.
Row 5: Knit.
Row 6: Yo, k2tog, knit until 3 stitches remain, wrap and turn.
Row 7: Knit.
Row 8: Yo, k2tog, knit to end of row.
Row 9: Knit.
Row 10: Yo, k2tog, knit to end of row.
Row 11: Knit.
Row 12 (increase row): Yo, knit to end of row.

Repeat short row wedge 2A 4 more times (5 repeats total) [35 stitches].

Section 4 - Central Wedge (22 rows, 11 loops)

Row 1: Knit.
Row 2: Yo, k2tog, knit until 11 stitches remain, wrap and turn.

Row 3: Knit.
Row 4: Yo, k2tog, knit until 7 stitches remain, wrap and turn.
Row 5: Knit.
Row 6: Yo, k2tog, knit until 3 stitches remain, wrap and turn.
Row 7, 9, 11, 13, 15: Knit.
Row 8, 10, 12, 14, 16: Yo, k2tog, knit to end of row.
Row 17: Knit.
Row 18: Yo, k2tog, knit until 3 stitches remain, wrap and turn.
Row 19: Knit.
Row 20: Yo, k2tog, knit until 7 stitches remain, wrap and turn.
Row 21: Knit.
Row 22: Yo, k2tog, knit until 11 stitches remain, wrap and turn [35 stitches].

Section 5 - Short Row Wedge 2B (60 rows, 30 loops)

Row 1: Knit.
Row 2 (decrease row): Yo, k3tog, knit to end of row.
Row 3: Knit.
Row 4: Yo, k2tog, knit to end of row.
Row 5: Knit.
Row 6: Yo, k2tog, knit to end of row.
Row 7: Knit.
Row 8: Yo, k2tog, knit until 3 stitches remain, wrap and turn.
Row 9: Knit.
Row 10: Yo, k2tog, knit until 7 stitches remain, wrap and turn.
Row 11: Knit.
Row 12: Yo, k2tog, knit until 11 stitches remain, wrap and turn.

Chart 1

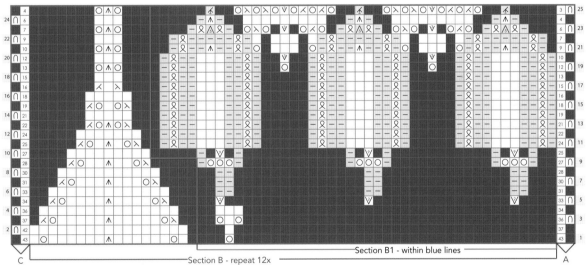

Section B - repeat 12x

Section B1 - within blue lines

NOTE: *The right and left side of the chart (section A and section C) have numbers in boxes. These boxes indicate to work that many stitches before or after working the chart. At the end of each row,* **make sure to work only the number indicated in the box** *before turning (except on the very first row), you will be leaving some stitches unworked on the needle as you work these short rows. Note that the numbers are decreasing as you go up and you slip the first stitch after every turn; this is creating tapered short row "wings" on each side of the edging.*

■	no stitch
□	k on RS, p on WS
−	p on RS, k on WS
ℛ	ktbl on RS, ptbl on WS
○	yo

⟋	k2tog
⟍	ssk
⟋	p3tog
⋀	cdd, p3tog on WS
⟑	p3tog, p2tog, pass 2nd stitch over 1st

Ⅴ	make 2 from 1 = [k, p] into same stitch
Ⅴ	make 3 from 1 = [k, p, k] into same stitch
Ⅴ	make 9 from 1 = [k, p, k, p, k, p, k, p, k] into same stitch
43	k on RS, p on WS the number of stitches indicated in the box
∩	slip stitch purlwise

Repeat short row wedge 2B 4 more times (5 repeats total) [30 stitches].

Section 6 - Short Row Wedge 1B (72 rows, 36 loops)

Row 1: Knit.
Row 2 (decrease row): Yo, k3tog, knit to end of row.
Row 3: Knit.
Row 4: Yo, k2tog, knit to end of row.
Row 5: Knit.
Row 6: Yo, k2tog, knit to end of row.
Row 7: Knit.
Row 8: Yo, k2tog, knit until 3 stitches remain, wrap and turn.

Repeat short row wedge 1B 8 more times (9 repeats total) [21 stitches].

Section 7 - Tail Wing B (144 rows, 72 loops)

Row 1: Knit.
Row 2 (decrease row): Yo, k3tog, knit to end of row.
Row 3: Knit.
Row 4: Yo, k2 tog, knit to end of row.
Row 5: Knit.
Row 6: Yo, k2tog, knit to end of row.
Row 7: Knit.
Row 8: Yo, k2tog, knit to end of row.

Repeat rows 1-8 until you have decreased 18 times [3 stitches]. Work 6 more rows of garter stitch, working yo, k2tog at the beginning of each RS row. You now have 290 loops. Bind off the 3 stitches and pull yarn through last loop without cutting yarn.

edging NOTE: *The right and left side of the chart (section A and section C) have numbers in boxes. These boxes indicate to work that many stitches before or after working the chart. At the end of each row, make sure to work only the number indicated in the box before turning, except on the very first row, you will be leaving some stitches unworked on the needle as you work these short rows. Note that the numbers are decreasing as you go up and you slip the first stitch after every turn; this is creating tapered short row "wings" on each side of the edging.*

Pick up and purl 290 stitches through the edge loops formed by the yos.

Follow chart 1 beginning at section A. When you have worked across section A, work section B 12 times, then work section B1 (the portion between the blue lines) once. Thereafter work section C.

When chart is finished at row 25, continue all the way to end of stitches in stockinette (across short rows). Work 3 rows of garter stitch across entire edging.

bind-off Bind off in the following method: [p2tog, slip stitch from right hand needle back to left hand needle], repeat until all stitches are bound off. Cut thread and pull remaining tail through last stitch.

finishing Weave in ends. Block on mat, pinning out points.

13. SKY BLUE

sizes Women's small (women's medium / men's small, women's large / men's medium, men's large). Size is determined by yarn size and needle size. Sample shown in size small.

yarn Fingering, sport, dk or worsted weight sock yarn, approximately 250 (200, 175, 150) yards [229 (183, 160, 137) meters].

Sample shown in Alisha Goes Around, Tiding (of Magpies), (63% Fine superwash merino wool, 15% silk, 10% nylon, 2% sterling silver floss), 420 yds (384 m) per 100 g in color "Seaglass."

needles US 2 (4, 6, 8) / 2.75 (3.5, 4, 5) mm or size needed to obtain gauge in circular or double point.

gauge 6.5 (5.5, 5, 4) stitches / 9 (7.5, 7, 5.5) rows per inch (2.5 cm) in 2 x 2 ribbing.

notions Stitch markers, stitch holder, cable needle, tapestry needle.

notes *Because linen stitch has little compression/stretch and rib has a lot of compression/stretch, work linen stitch loosely and ribs snugly. If needed you may adjust needle size.*
Stitches are divided into two categories, back of hand (from here on referred to as "back") and palm of hand (from here on referred to as "palm").

cast-on Using the cast-on of your choice, cast on 48 stitches. Divide evenly between needles and join to begin working in the round, being careful not to twist stitches when joining. If needed, place marker to indicate the beginning of the round.

cuff
Left Mitt
Rounds 1-12: Beginning with p, work p2, k2 ribbing across all stitches.

Right Mitt
Rounds 1-12: Beginning with k, work k2, p2 ribbing across all stitches.

arm
Left Mitt
Rounds 1-22: Beginning with back of hand, work rows 1-24 of chart 1 (left).

Round 23: Work row 25 of chart 1 (left), noting that the cable cross happens on the first 2 palm stitches and the last 2 back stitches. Slip the first two stitches and work across chart1 (left).

When you reach the last two stitches, slip the first two palm stitches to your back needle to perform the cross, then slip them back to the palm needle.

Rounds 24-46: Continue following chart 1 (left).

Round 47: Work row 47 of chart 1 (left), noting that the cable cross happens on the last 2 palm stitches and the first 2 back stitches, so you may have to temporarily rearrange your stitches to accommodate this.

Rounds 48-70: Work rows 48-70 of chart 1 (left).

Right Mitt:

Work as for left mitt, substituting chart 1 (right) for chart 1 (left).

thumb gusset You will continue to work the linen stitch and rib pattern as established while making increases for your thumb. The thumb stitches will be worked in reverse stockinette stitch.

Left Mitt:
Round 1: Work as established until last 4 stitches of row, k2, place marker, m1R, yo, place marker, k2.

Right Mitt:
Round 1: K2, place marker, m1R, yo, place marker, k2, work in pattern as established until the end of the round.

Both Mitts:
Round 2: Work as established until first marker, slip marker, purl to next marker, slip marker, k2, continue as established until the end of the round.
Round 3: Work as established until first marker, slip marker, m1R, purl to next marker purling through the back of the yo from the previous round, m1L, slip marker, k2, continue as established until the end of the Round.
Round 4: Work as established until first marker, slip marker, purl to next marker, slip marker, k2, continue as established until the end of the round.

Chart 1 (left)   (palm)   (back of hand)

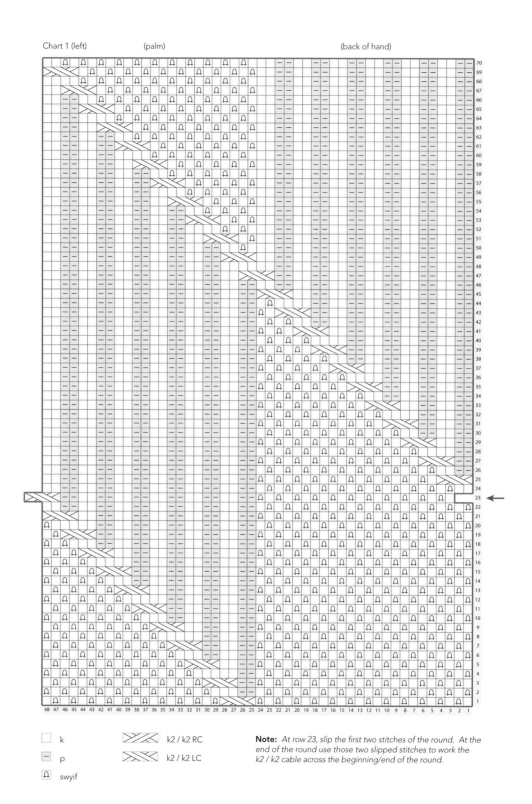

	k		k2 / k2 RC
	p		k2 / k2 LC
	swyif		

Note: At row 23, slip the first two stitches of the round. At the end of the round use those two slipped stitches to work the k2 / k2 cable across the beginning/end of the round.

Chart 1 (right)   (back of hand)   (palm)

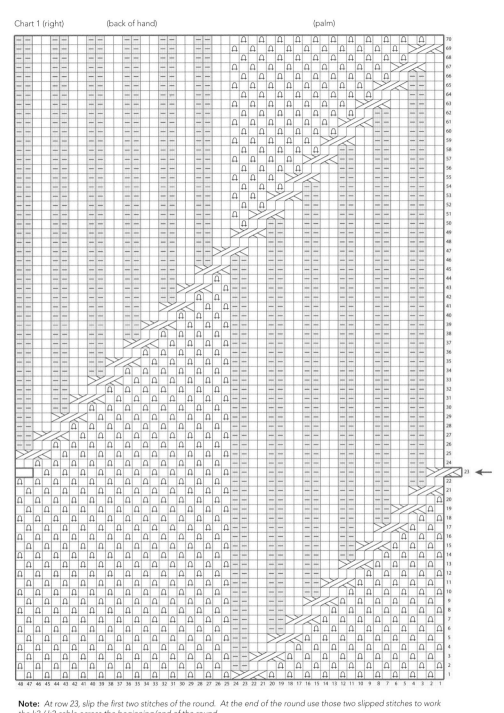

Note: *At row 23, slip the first two stitches of the round. At the end of the round use those two slipped stitches to work the k2 / k2 cable across the beginning/end of the round.*

Repeat Rounds 3-4 until there are 20 (16, 14, 12) thumb stitches between markers.

Left Mitt:

Work as established until first marker, slip marker, slip thumb stitches onto stitch holder, remove next marker, cast on 2 stitches, k2.

Next Round: Work as established until first marker, slip marker, p2, k2.

Repeat this last round for 0.5" or until 1.75" less than desired length.

Right Mitt:

Knit 2, slip marker, slip thumb stitches onto stitch holder, remove next marker, cast on 2 stitches, k2, place marker, continue as established until the end of the round.

Next Round: Knit 2, slip marker, p2, k2, slip marker, continue as established until the end of the round.

Repeat this last round for 0.5" or until 1.75" less than desired length.

Left Mitt:

Round 1: Work in pattern as established until 2 stitches before marker, slip 2 stitches to cable needle and hold in front, remove marker, p2tog twice (removing second marker), k2 from cable needle.

Rounds 2 - 15: [P2, k2] across all stitches.

Right Mitt:

Round 1: Knit 2, slip 4 stitches to cable needle and hold back, k2, [p2tog] twice from cable needle, (k2, p2) until end of round.

Rounds 2 - 15: [K2, p2] across all stitches.

bind-off Bind off all stitches loosely in pattern, using a sewn bind off or some other stretchy bind off of your choice.

thumb Slide the stitches on hold to working needles and divide to work in the round. Attach yarn, leaving a long tail to sew up holes later, and purl across. Pick up and purl 4 stitches along the hand side of the mitt.

Rounds 1-3: Purl around all stitches.
Rounds 4-10: Work linen stitch pattern across all stitches.

Bind off as described above.

finishing Weave in ends. Use long tail at thumb to sew up any holes. Block as desired.

Because of the different texture of the stitches, the mitt will bias a bit off the hand. It will fit well when worn.

14. ZIGZAG WANDERER

sizes One size. Gauge and blocking will affect finished size.

yarn Fingering weight sock yarn, approximately 400 yds (366 m).

Green scarf shown in Malabrigo Sock Yarn (100% superwash merino), 440 yds (402 m) per 100 g in color "Lettuce."

needles US 5 / 3.75 mm or size needed to obtain gauge.

gauge 6 stitches / 9 rows per inch (2.54 cm) in stockinette, blocked.

notions Tapestry needle.

68 in (173 cm)

8 in (20 cm)

Chart 1

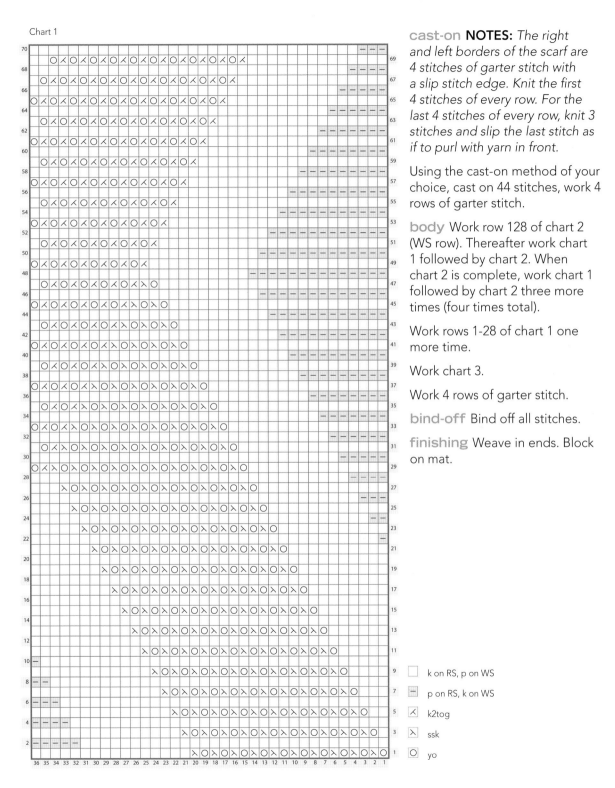

cast-on **NOTES:** *The right and left borders of the scarf are 4 stitches of garter stitch with a slip stitch edge. Knit the first 4 stitches of every row. For the last 4 stitches of every row, knit 3 stitches and slip the last stitch as if to purl with yarn in front.*

Using the cast-on method of your choice, cast on 44 stitches, work 4 rows of garter stitch.

body Work row 128 of chart 2 (WS row). Thereafter work chart 1 followed by chart 2. When chart 2 is complete, work chart 1 followed by chart 2 three more times (four times total).

Work rows 1-28 of chart 1 one more time.

Work chart 3.

Work 4 rows of garter stitch.

bind-off Bind off all stitches.

finishing Weave in ends. Block on mat.

☐ k on RS, p on WS

− p on RS, k on WS

⟋ k2tog

⟍ ssk

○ yo

Chart 2

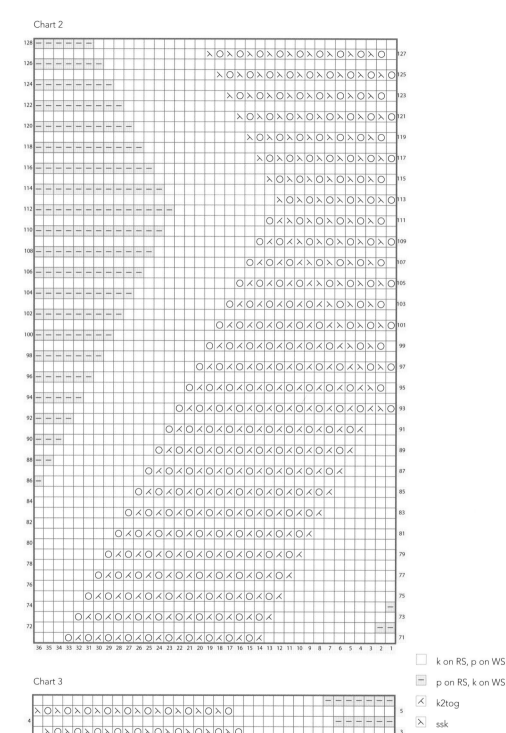

	k on RS, p on WS
—	p on RS, k on WS
⊼	k2tog
λ	ssk
O	yo

Chart 3

15. BIVALVE

sizes Small (large). Gauge and blocking will affect finished size. Size small shown in lavender; size large shown in grey.

yarn Fingering weight sock yarn, approximately 320 (485) yds (293 (444) m).

Lavender shawlette shown in Alpha B Yarn, Luxe B (50% superwash merino, 50% silk), 427 yds (309 m) per 100 g in color "The World is my Oyster."

Grey shawl shown in Socktopus Sokkusu O for Original sock yarn (100% superwash merino), 433 yds (396 m) per 120 g in color "Man of Rock."

needles US 8 / 5 mm or size needed to obtain gauge.

gauge 3 stitches / 5 rows per inch (2.54 cm) in lace pattern.

notions Stitch markers, tapestry needle.

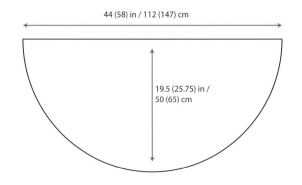

44 (58) in / 112 (147) cm

19.5 (25.75) in / 50 (65) cm

cast-on NOTE: *The shawl is worked from the center top downward and outward, starting with a garter tab. Any provisional cast-on may be used for beginning the garter tab.*

Using a provisional cast-on, cast on 2 stitches. Work 8 rows garter st.

Turn the work 90 degrees so that the edge of the garter strip is now at the top and the live stitches are on the right hand side. Pick up and knit 1 stitch in each of the 4 purl bumps along the edge of the garter strip. Place the 2 held stitches on a needle and knit them [8 stitches].

body NOTE: *When working into the double yarn overs on the following rows, treat each yarn over as a separate stitch.*

Row 1 (RS): K2, [kfb] 4 times, k2 [12 stitches].
Row 2 (WS): K2, p8, k2.
Row 3: K2, [kfb] 8 times, k2 [20 stitches].
Row 4: K2, p16, k2.
Row 5: Knit.
Row 6: K2, [place marker, p2] 8 times, place marker, k2.

Knit 2 stitches, [slip marker, work chart 1], repeat 8 times, slip marker, k2.
Working in this way, work rows 1-24 of chart 1 one time [68 stitches].

NOTE: *The red box on chart two is the repeat area. Work this box 1 time per section on the first repeat of the chart, 3 times the second repeat and 5 times on the third repeat of the chart. The entire chart is worked 8 times across on each row.*

Knit 2 stitches, [slip marker, work chart 2], repeat 8 times, slip maker, k2.
Working in this way, work rows 1-32 of chart 2 one (two) time(s) [132 (196) stitches].
Work rows 1-16 one more time [164 (228) stitches].

Remove the markers on the last body row.

border **Set up for border (RS):** K2, [kfb, k18 (26), kfb], repeat 8 times, k2 [180 (244) stitches].

NOTES: *Chart 3 (border pattern) is knit onto the live body stitches. The last stitch of each WS row is knit together with the next live stitch on the body. The stitch count on chart 3 changes throughout. Chart 3 starts with a wrong side row.*

Using a knitted cast-on, cast on an additional 13 stitches.

Row 1(WS): Knit 12, knit the 13th stitch together with the first live stitch on the body of the shawl.
Row 2 (RS): Knit 13.

Work rows 1-2 a total of 2 (3) times.

Work rows 1-14 of the border chart 25 (34) times, knitting the last stitch of all WS rows together with the next stitch on the body of the shawl.

Row 1 (WS): Knit 12, knit the 13th stitch together with the first live stitch on the body of the shawl.
Row 2 (RS): Knit 13.

Work rows 1-2 a total of 2 times.

Work row 1 one more time.

bind-off Bind off the remaining 13 stitches.

finishing Weave in ends. Block on mat, pinning out points.

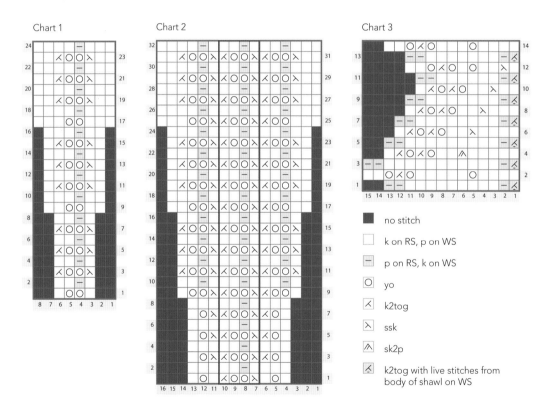

NOTES: *The red box on chart 2 is the repeat area. Work this box 1 time in each section on the first repeat of the chart, 3 times on the second repeat and 5 times on the third repeat of the chart.*

16. CASSIAN

sizes One size, gauge and blocking will affect size.

yarn Fingering weight sock yarn, approximately 575 yds (525 m).

Sample shown in Pigeonroof Studios Siren Two Sock (80% superwash merino wool, 10% cashmere, 10% nylon) 380 yds (347 m) per 100 gr in color "Inkpot," 2 skeins.

needles US 6 (4 mm) circular needle, or size needed to obtain gauge.

gauge 6 stitches / 7 rows per inch (2.54 cm) in lace pattern worked flat after blocking. Correct gauge is not critical for this project but your final measurements and yardage requirements may vary if your gauge is different.

notions Stitch markers, tapestry needle.

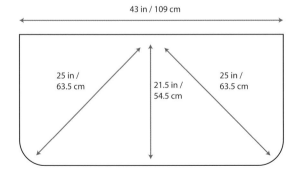

43 in / 109 cm

25 in / 63.5 cm

21.5 in / 54.5 cm

25 in / 63.5 cm

notes *This pattern is started with a small cast-on (33 sts), which is sewn together after the shawl is completed. After the set-up section, the increases are worked in two sections on each side of the shawl. The first 3 sts of the set-up section have short-row shaping to keep the sts in the center of the shawl from bunching up.*

All double yarnovers are worked as (k1, p1) on the subsequent rows.

The buttercup lace pattern in the panels has changing stitch counts - it starts with 5 sts and goes up to 15 sts. If desired, additional stitch markers can be used to mark off the lace panels and the edging, but use different color or style markers for the markers used in the instructions, as the directions are written using those markers as points of reference.

This shawl can be easily be made larger or smaller. Just make sure to finish on row 8 or 16 before beginning the final edging.

cast-on Cast on 33 stitches, leaving a long tail that can used to sew together the cast-on edge after finishing the shawl. Work the 8-row set-up section using either the written instructions or chart 1. After the set-up section is completed, there will be 51 stitchess on the needles. Place markers as follows: work 7 stitches, place marker, work 13 stitches, place marker, work 1 stitch, place marker, work 13 stitches, place marker, work 1 stitch, place marker, work 13 stitches, place marker.

setup

Row 1 (RS): K5, yo, k2tog, k1, yo, k1, yo, (k yo k) in 1, yo, k1, yo, k3, yo, k2tog, (k yo k) in 1, k2, yo, k2tog, k1, yo, k1, yo, (k yo k) in 1, yo, k1, yo, k3, yo, k2tog, turn - 3 sts remain on the needles.

Row 2 (WS): K2, yo, k2tog, p11, k2, yo, k2tog, p3, k2, yo, k2tog, p11, k2, yo, k2tog, turn - 3 sts remain on the needles.

Row 3: K2, yo, k2tog, k1, yo, k3, yo, k3, yo, k3, yo, k3, yo, k2tog, k1, yo, (k yo k) in 1, yo, k3, yo, k2tog, k1, yo, k3, yo, k3, yo, k3, yo, k3, yo, k2tog, k3.

Row 4: K5, yo, k2tog, p6, p3tog, p6, k2, yo, k2tog, p7, k2, yo, k2tog, p6, p3tog, p6, k2, yo, k2tog, k1, yo2, k1, yo2, k1.

Row 5: K2, p1, k2, p1, k3, yo, k2tog, k1, yo, ssk, k1, k2tog, yo, k1, yo, ssk, k1, k2tog, yo, k3, yo, k2tog, k1, yo, k1, yo, k3, yo, k1, yo, k3, yo, k2tog, k1, yo, ssk, k1, k2tog, yo, k1, yo, ssk, k1, k2tog, yo, k3, yo, k2tog, k1, yo2, k1, yo2, k1.

Row 6: K2, p1, k2, p1, k3, yo, k2tog, p1, p2tog, p1, ssp, p1, p2tog, p1, ssp, p1, k2, yo, k2tog, p11, k2, yo, k2tog, p1, p2tog, p1, ssp, p1, p2tog, p1, ssp, p1, k2, yo, k2tog, k7.

Row 7: Bind off 4, k4, yo, k2tog, k1, yo, sk2p, k1, k3tog, yo, k3, yo, k2tog, k1, yo, k2tog , yo, k1, yo, sk2p, yo, k1, yo, ssk, yo, k3, yo, k2tog, k1, yo, sk2p, k1, k3tog, yo, k3, yo, k2tog, k8.

Row 8: Bind off 4, k4, yo, k2tog, p2, p3tog, p2, k2, yo, k2tog, p1, k2, yo, p6, k2, yo, p2, k2, yo, k2tog, p2, p3tog, p2, k2, yo, k2tog, k1, yo2, k1, yo2, k1.

increase repeats Work the 16-row increase repeat following chart 2. Each increase repeat adds 36 sts to the total stitch count. After the first increase repeat, there will be 87 sts on the needles. After each repeat, move the increase section stitch markers as follows – there will be 19 sts in each increase section, move the markers so that the center stitch is marked off only – ready to work the next repeat. Work a total of six increase repeats [267 sts]. To change size of shawl, work either more or fewer repeats of chart 2.

lace edging Remove all stitch markers. The first 11 sts on the needle are the lace edging that will be applied around the bottom of the shawl - the lace edging repeat is 4 rows long. The edging is attached to the live stitches on the bottom of the shawl by working a k3tog. To turn the corner, the edging will be attached 4 times (two full repeats) to the corner before continuing to attach it to the live sts. Before starting the lace edging, pick up 4 sts in the corner of the shawl very close together.

Row 1: K2, p1, k2, p1, k3, yo, k3tog using 1 live stitch from the shawl.
Row 2: Slip 1, k1, yo, k2tog, k7.
Row 3: Bind off 4, k4, yo, k3tog using 1 live stitch from the shawl.
Row 4: Slip 1, k1, yo, k2tog, k1, yo2, k1, yo2, k1.

Continue in this manner, working one live stitch from the shawl together with the lace edging using a k3tog on every right side row, until 7 sts remain - the lace edging from the other end of the shawl. Pick up 4 sts in the last corner very close together the same way as the first corner. Work 7 more rows of the lace, edging off the last 4 corner sts. If the final row is row 4 of the lace edging, DO NOT work the double yos - there will now be 14 sts on the needles. If the final row is row 2, work as directed, but before grafting, bind off 4 sts so that there are only 7 sts on each side. Use the kitchener stitch to graft the 7 sts from the bottom lace edging to the 7 sts from the top edging of the shawl.

finishing Weave in all ends. Sew cast-on edge together carefully, matching up the lace pattern so that it flows using mattress stitch. Soak shawl and wet block into a half-circle/crescent shape, using pins or wires as desired.

Chart 1

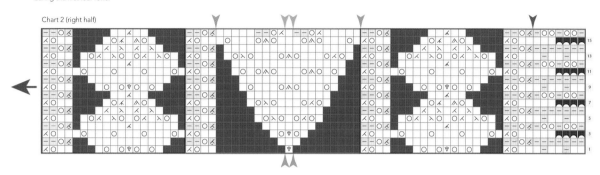

NOTE:
The stitches marked in yellow in chart 1 are not worked during the first four rows.

Chart 2 (right half)

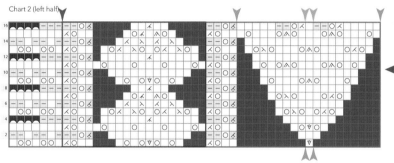

Chart 2 (left half)

NOTE: *Chart 2 is broken into two sections! Begin with the right half above and continue along the left half when you reach the red arrow.*

NOTE:
Red boxes indicate pattern repeats. Arrowheads indicate stitch marker placement. Green arrowheads at the bottom of chart 2 show the original position of these markers. As you work through the chart the stitches expand between the markers so that they are in the position shown at the top at the end of the chart. At the end of each repeat of the chart, remove these green markers and place them in the orange position (which is the same as the green position at the bottom of the chart) so they will be in position for the next repeat of the chart. Each time you begin row 1 of chart 2, you will have added one repeat at each outside edge, and two more in the center.

■ no stitch	⅄ cdd
⊤ k on RS, p on WS	⅄ p2tog on RS, k2tog on WS
− p on RS, k on WS	♈ kyok
⋌ k2tog on RS, p2tog on WS	⅄ k3 tog on RS, p3tog on WS
⋋ ssk on RS, ssp on WS	⅄ sk2p
○ yo	■ bind off

Abbreviations and Glossary
Techniques required

Wrap and turn
Icord
Knitted cast-on
Provisional cast-on
Judy's magic cast-on
Jeny's surprisingly stretchy bind-off
Kitchener stitch
Crochet bind-off

Tutorials for these techniques can be found on our website thesockreport.com

■	no stitch	ignore these boxes, they are placeholders
□	k	knit
—	p	purl
ktbl	ktbl	knit through back loop
	ptbl	purl through back loop
∩	slip stitch purlwise	slip stitch as if to purl
⋔	swyif	slip stitch with yarn in front
↷	psso	pass slipped stitch over - in this pattern this stitch is used at the end of a round, where the last stitch of the round is not worked, but passed over the first stitch of the round (which was a k2tog) resulting in a double decrease.
⟋	k2tog	knit two together
⟍	ssk	slip, slip, knit
⟋	k2tog tbl	knit two together through the back loop
⟍	ssk tbl	slip, slip, knit through the back loop
⟋	k3tog	knit three together

⟍	sssk	slip, slip, slip, knit
⟋	p2tog	purl two together
⟋	p3tog	purl three together
	ssp	slip, slip purl
	RS	right side
	WS	wrong side
⋀	cdd	centered double decrease; slip 2 stitches together knit-wise, knit the next stitch, pass the 2 slipped stitches over.
⋀	sk2p	slip one, k2tog, pass slipped stitch over
⋀	decrease 5 to 1	p3tog, p2tog, pass second stitch over first stitch.
O	yo	yarn over
	kfb	knit into the front and back of stitch
ℛ	m1R	make 1 by inserting the left-hand needle under the bar between your stitches from back to front, knit through the front
ℛ	m1L	make 1 by inserting the left-hand needle under the bar between your stitches from front to back, knit through the back
	pfb	purl into the front and back of same stitch.
ℛ	m1R purl-wise	with left needle, lift strand between needles from back to front and purl through front
ℛ	m1L purl-wise	with left needle, lift strand between needles from front to back and purl tbl

Symbol	Name	Description
Y	Rli	right leaning increase. Make 1 by knitting into the right leg of the stitch below the next stitch.
Y	Lli	left leaning increase. Make 1 by knitting into the left leg of the stitch below the one you just knit.
ⱱ	kyok	knit, yo, knit in the same stitch.
ⱱ	special increase	Make two stitches from 1 by knitting into each separate strand of a double stranded stitch.
V₂	make 2 from 1	[k, p] into same stitch
V₃	make 3 from 1	[k, p, k] into same stitch
V₉	make 9 from 1	[k, p, k, p, k, p, k, p, k] into same stitch
43	knit this number of stitches	knit the number of stitches indicated inside box.
↓	drop stitch	drop the next stitch off the needle and let it ladder down to the yo. The yo will stop the ladder.
▨	knit slipped stitch	knit the slipped stitch from below
▨	k, wrap 3x	knit, wrapping yarn 3x around needle,this stitch will be slipped on subsequent rows until it is shown to knit it.
▨	knit slipped stitch + k wrap 3x	knit the slipped stitch from below, while at the same time wrapping yarn 3x around needle to create a new slipped stitch.
╲		shows slipped stitch origin and destination

Symbol	Name	Description
⊏⊐	wrap 3 stitches	Slip 3 stitches with yarn in back, move yarn to front, slip the same 3 stitches back, move yarn to back and cinch.
╱	k1 / k1 RC	slip 1 stitch to cable needle, hold in back, knit the next stitch, knit the stitch from cable needle.
╲	k1 / k1 LC	slip 1 stitch to cable needle, hold in front, knit the next stitch, knit the stitch from cable needle.
╱	k1tbl / k1 RC	slip 1 stitch to cable needle, hold in back, knit the next stitch through the back loop, knit the stitch from cable needle.
╲	k1tbl / k1 LC	slip 1 stitch to cable needle, hold in front, knit the next stitch, knit the stitch from cable needle through the back loop.
╱	k1 / p1 RC	slip 1 stitch to cable needle, hold in back, knit the next stitch, purl the stitch from cable needle.
╲	k1 / p1 LC	slip 1 stitch to cable needle, hold in front, purl the next stitch, knit the stitch from cable needle.
╱	k1 tbl / p1 RC	slip 1 stitch to cable needle, hold in back, knit the next stitch through the back loop, purl the stitch from cable needle.
╲	k1 tbl / p1 LC	slip 1 stitch to cable needle, hold in front, purl the next stitch, knit the stitch from cable needle through the back loop.

	k2 / p2 RC	slip 2 stitches to cable needle, hold in back, knit the next 2 stitches, purl the 2 stitches from cable needle.
	k2 / p2 LC	slip 2 stitches to cable needle, hold in front, purl the next 2 stitches, knit the 2 stitches from cable needle.
	k2 / p1 RC	slip 1 stitch to cable needle, hold in back, knit the next 2 stitches, purl the stitch from cable needle.
	k2 / p1 LC	slip 2 stitches to cable needle, hold in front, purl the next stitch, knit the 2 stitches from cable needle.
	k2 / p1 / k2 LC	slip 3 stitches to cable needle, hold in front, knit the next 2 stitches, slip last stitch from cable needle, purl 1, knit 2 stitches from cable needle.
	k1 tbl / p1 / k1 tbl RC	see notes on chart key.
	k2 / k2 RC	slip 2 stitches to cable needle, held in back. Knit the next 2 stitches. Knit 2 stitches from cable needle.
	k2 / k2 LC	slip 2 stitches to cable needle held in front. Knit the next 2 stitches. Knit 2 stitches from cable needle.
	k1 tbl / p3 RC	slip 3 stitches to cable needle, hold in back, knit the next stitch throught the back loop, purl the 3 stitches from cable needle.

	k1 tbl / p3 LC	slip 1 stitch to cable needle, hold in front, purl the next 3 stitches, knit the stitch from cable needle through the back loop.
	k1 / k2 k1 tbl RC	slip 3 stitches to cable needle, hold in back, knit the next stitch, knit 2 stitches from cable needle, knit last stitck from cable needle through the back loop.
	k1 / k2 k1 tbl LC	slip 1 stitch to cable needle, hold in front, knit the next stitch through the back loop, knit the next 2 stitches, knit the stitch from cable needle
	k1 / k1 RC with k2tog	slip 1 stitch to right needle, slip next to cable needle, hold in back, slip the next stitch to right needle, knit the stitch from cable needle, slip the 2 slipped stitches back to left needle and k2tog.
	bind-off	bind off
	nupp	k1, yo, k1, yo, k1 in same stitch. Turn (WS facing). Insert needle through all loops and knit all 5 stitches together. Turn (RS facing).
	bead	bead is placed on stitch by sliding bead onto small crochet hook, then slipping stitch from needle to crochet hook and drawing through the center of the bead. Replace stitch on left needle and work according to pattern.

Editor in Chief	Janel Laidman
Art Design	Janel Laidman
Stylist	Annabel Percy
Technical Editing	Miriam Pike
	Susan Moskwa
	Cathy Berry
	Kris Redmond
Production	Janel Laidman
	Miriam Pike
	Annabel Percy
Photography	Benjamin Wheeler
	Janel Laidman
Photo Assistants	Sarah Etherton
	Amanda Haugland
Models	Miriam Pike
	Annabel Percy

The Sock Report, vol 1, summer 2012

The Sock Report is published by Rustling Leaf Press, P.O. Box 21805 Eugene, OR 97402. All contents are copyright Rustling Leaf Press, 2012.

The Sock Report is currently published twice a year in Spring and Fall. Our sister publication, **Skein Theory**, is published in early Autumn and Winter.

COLOPHON

The Sock Report text is set in Avenir LT Std Light & Heavy

Special typefaces: Bickham Script, English Script, Anglican, Century Handtooled ITC Std, Trade Gothic LT Std.

Special Thanks To:

Sokkusu Yarn & Patterns
Blue Moon Fiber Arts
Cephalopod Yarns
Signature Needles
Indigo Moon
Hazel Knits
Huckleberry Knits
Sweet Georgia Yarns
Three Fates Yarns
Plymouth Yarn
Handwerks Artisan Yarns & Textiles
Knot Another Hat
Lorna's Laces
Textiles a Mano
Alpha B Yarns
Ravelry

Our Test Knitters

100 Creations
Bellarose4
bwarnergroup
Caillean
curiouskate
dclulu
figment49
hautepoet
houghmary
jnelson8705
joandyer

KnitnGlo
knitterloreen
lampi
love2read
LuckyLindey
Lucybeth
Lumberjill
lynndicristina
mickieswall
nephele
nightandday

oslogirl
racoonims
sarahsh123
seeingeyeknitter
sockalicious
sockpirate
stebo79
thehulkstoy
WendyJoJo
Wool4willow

Our Designers

Susanna IC - ArtQualia.com
Miriam Pike
AnneLena Mattison
Snowden Becker - tt820classyknitting.blogspot.com
Chris deLongpre - KnittingatKnoon.com
Laura Kanemori - mytinkertots.blogspot.com
Heatherly Walker - yarnyenta.com
Kristi Geraci
Friederike Erbslein
Hunter Hammersen - violentlydomestic.com
Janel Laidman - janellaidman.com
Star Athena - keeponknittinginthe freeworld.blogspot.com
Kimley Maretzo - kimleyknits.com
Kirsten Kapur- throughtheloops.typepad.com
Corinna Ferguson

Photographs ©2012, Benjamin Wheeler and Rustling Leaf Press

Marigold ©2012, Rustling Leaf Press and Susanna IC
Suki©2012, Rustling Leaf Press and Miriam Pike
Blomster, Tulip Dreams, ©2012, Rustling Leaf Press and AnneLena Mattison
Clio, ©2012, Rustling Leaf Press and Snowden Becker
Devonian, ©2012, Rustling Leaf Press and Laura Kanemori
Semadar, ©2012, Rustling Leaf Press and Heatherly Walker
Cambium, ©2012, Rustling Leaf Press and Kristi Geraci
Wanderlust, ©2012, Rustling Leaf Press and Friederike Erbslein
Phaeodaria, ©2012, Rustling Leaf Press and Hunter Hammersen
Arcadia, ©2012, Rustling Leaf Press and Janel Laidman
Sky Blue, ©2012, Rustling Leaf Press and Star Athena
Zigzag Wanderer, ©2012, Rustling Leaf Press and Kimley Maretzo
Bivalve, ©2012, Rustling Leaf Press and Kirsten Kapur
Cassian, ©2012, Rustling Leaf Press and Corrina Ferguson

First published 2012 by Rustling Leaf Press

Printed and bound in U.S. by Versa Press

ISBN-13: 978-0-9814972-5-9